FOR
REFERENCE ONLY

MANAGING IN BRITAIN AND GERMANY

Managing in Britain and Germany

Rosemary Stewart

Jean-Louis Barsoux

Alfred Kieser

Hans-Dieter Ganter

and

Peter Walgenbach

St. Martin's Press

First published in Great Britain 1994 by
THE MACMILLAN PRESS LTD
Houndmills, Basingstoke, Hampshire RG21 2XS
and London
Companies and representatives
throughout the world

A catalogue record for this book is available
from the British Library.

ISBN 0–333–60646–9

Printed in Great Britain by
Antony Rowe Ltd
Chippenham, Wiltshire

First published in the United States of America 1994 by
Scholarly and Reference Division,
ST. MARTIN'S PRESS, INC.,
175 Fifth Avenue,
New York, N.Y. 10010

ISBN 0–312–12237–3

Library of Congress Cataloging-in-Publication Data
Managing in Britain and Germany / Rosemary Stewart . . . [et al.].
p.   cm.
Includes bibliographical references and index.
ISBN 0–312–12237–3
1. Management—Great Britain. 2. Management—Germany.
3. Executives—Great Britain. 4. Executives—Germany. 5. Corporate
culture—Great Britain. 6. Corporate culture—Germany.
I. Stewart, Rosemary.
HD70.G7M328 1994
658'.00941—dc20   94–20536
                                                   CIP

Contents

List of Figures

List of Tables

Acknowledgements

The British side of the research was funded by the Anglo–German Foundation. We are grateful for the financial support, and to Connie Martin and Ray Cunningham for their helpful approach throughout the study which made the work of the British pair much easier.

We are also much indebted to Gerd Junginger for his illuminating translation and commentary on the German interviews. To this he brought his experience of working in a large company both in Britain and Germany. We benefited from the support of colleagues and facilities at Templeton College. In particular, our colleague Sue Dopson was of much help in the early stages of planning the project. Val Martin, Lorraine Matthews and Maggie Latham provided invaluable help with presentational input. The latter efficiently and cheerfully did the dreary late stages of getting the book ready for the publisher. A two-country, multi-authored book makes this even harder than usual. The British researchers are indebted to their German colleagues for their fluent English.

The German part of this research project received a grant by the Deutsche Forschungsgemeinschaft. It also benefited from the support of the Center for European Economic Research, Mannheim.

Both British and German authors are most grateful to the companies which agreed to take part in the research and to the managers who gave their time and experience to cooperate in the research.

R. S.
J.-L. B.
A. K.
H.-D. G.
P. W.

Introduction

RATIONALE OF THE STUDY

In this report we present the results of empirical research into the roles and behaviour of middle managers in British and German companies. The rationale behind this study can be explained by answering three questions. Why did we analyse the roles and behaviour of managers? Why did we analyse middle managers, not top managers? And, finally, why did we make it a cross-cultural comparison?

Why Another Study of Managerial Behaviour?

There are already many empirical studies available in which researchers have tried to find out what managers really do.[1] Many of these studies originated in the USA, with a seminal early study from Sweden and a variety of studies in Britain. Astonishingly though, we know very little about the behaviour of German managers who, in spite of their high profile in German society, have rarely been the object of empirical studies.

On the face of it, the existing empirical research on managerial behaviour has produced convergent results. For instance, it has established that the working day of a manager is highly fragmented, that it consists of many short episodes, and that the manager is often reacting to unscheduled events or to disturbances. Another finding, supported in many studies, is that managers often spend much of their time away from their own offices in other parts of the company or visiting other organizations. They also prefer oral to written communication.

In spite of this convergence of findings, there are still many things we do not know about managerial behaviour. First, the convergence only holds with regard to very crude tendencies. A closer look reveals significant differences between the behaviour patterns of managers at different levels, in different functions, companies, or countries. So far, we do not have satisfactory explanations for these differences. Existing studies are predominantly descriptive: they do not identify factors which can explain *why* managers in certain situations behave differently from managers in other situations. Therefore, it is necessary to base empirical analysis on improved concepts of managerial behaviour, and in our study we have tried to develop one such concept, as presented in Chapter 1. Also integrated into our framework are expectations of superiors and organizational structure – official job descriptions, the distribution of responsibilities, the coordination mechanisms and so on. These expectations have a strong impact on the behaviour of managers.

Second, as we point out in Chapter 1, existing empirical studies suffer from a number of methodological weaknesses. We have tried to overcome these by introducing new methodological approaches, which are described in Chapter 2.

Third, as previously mentioned, there are very few studies of this kind on German managers. In our own research we had severe difficulties in getting German managers to agree to observation. We think that this negative attitude towards observation is at least a partial explanation for the lack of studies on the behaviour of German managers – though lack of familiarity with the idea may also be an inhibiting factor. Many German researchers on managerial behaviour have simply assumed that the results from America and Britain were also valid for Germany.

Thus, our answer to the first question is that existing studies leave many questions unanswered. The answers can only be provided through improved conceptualization and methodology, as attempted in this study. Analysing management behaviour in Germany needs even less justification, because of the scarcity of existing material.

Why Middle Managers?

When a company is successful, top management gets all the praise and when it is unsuccessful, top management also gets all the blame. On the basis of this conventional wisdom almost all empirical studies on managerial behaviour have focused on top managers. Our interest in top managers was mainly in their capacity as superiors of middle managers, who were the main focus of this study.

The first reason for concentrating on middle managers was simply that they are still a largely unknown species. Implicitly, sometimes even explicitly, middle managers are assumed to be miniature versions of top managers. The assumption is that they basically have to perform the same functions, and that they have to behave in a similar way, if they are to be effective. The differences between top and middle managers are presumed to be differences of degree rather than differences in kind: their tasks are more structured and more limited in scope, as are their decision competences and responsibilities. If these assumptions hold, empirical results which are valid for top managers also roughly apply to middle managers.

In many studies the function of middle managers is likened to that of a transmission belt: they have to define decisions made by top managers, to break them down into subdecisions and, finally, to implement these subdecisions. Even if this view of the function of middle managers holds true, it does not necessarily mean that behaving like top managers is effective. Breaking down and implementing strategic decisions is different from making them and may require a different type of behaviour.

But what if the view of middle managers as transmission belts is inadequate? What if middle managers have to fulfil functions of another kind in addition to that of transforming top-management decisions into actions? Then the role of middle managers would be essentially different from those of top managers, and effective behaviour for them would differ from that of top managers. There are indications, that middle managers indeed have to fulfil functions which are different from those of top management. For instance, a few authors have posited that middle managers are responsible for preserving organizational knowledge[2] and for buffering the organization from internal and external shocks.[3] However, these authors do not empirically analyse to what extent and in what ways middle managers fulfil these functions, or if they do their findings may be dated.[4]

A final reason for concentrating on middle managers is that the influence of organizational structure and technology on managerial roles and behaviour can be expected to be stronger at this level than at the level of top management.

One of the aims of our study is therefore to consider to what extent and in which ways the roles and behaviour of middle managers replicate those of top managers. Empirical research on this issue seems of special significance given the ongoing debate about lean management. If middle management fulfils a function quite different from that of top management, then there may be risks attached to regarding most middle managers as dispensable. At least, programmes to implement lean management would have to make certain that the functions performed by middle management are somehow preserved.

Why Britain and Germany?

It is not necessary to go as far afield as Japan to find organizations significantly different from those in Britain and the USA. Even among the Western industrialized nations, one can find vastly divergent approaches to management. So far, comparative studies of organizations have concentrated on differences in organizational structures and management systems.

However, it can be assumed that management roles and behaviour are also different. By contrasting management roles in Britain and Germany, we hoped to contribute to the understanding of the impact of culture on organizations. Empirically supported knowledge in this field is not only of academic interest since cooperation between British and German managers will intensify, as a consequence of the increase in cross-border activity within the European Community. An awareness of how and why managerial behaviour in other cultures is different, will enhance communication and cooperation. Such knowledge may play a large role in the design and execution of joint ventures between British and German companies.

There is a further reason for making the study a cross-cultural one: through comparison it is possible to gain a better understanding of the patterns of managerial behaviour which prevail in the organizations within the two cultures. For instance, should we discover that certain management problems are solved differently in the two cultures, this will trigger the question: which factors are responsible for these differences? In this way, it may be possible to identify the relationship between managerial behaviour and national culture. Without a cross-cultural comparison it is much more difficult to identify and explain patterns of managerial behaviour, since there are no alternative patterns to provide a contrast. Such a comparison also allows us to speculate about the relative effectiveness of different patterns of managerial behaviour – and to consider whether the more effective solution can be transplanted into the other culture. Since direct transplantation is often impossible, it is necessary to design 'functional equivalences': that is, to find ways of reconciling the more effective pattern of behaviour with the local conditions of the host culture – in much the same way that 'quality circles' borrowed from Japan, had to be adapted to the needs and peculiarities of the Western organizations which adopted them.

Part I

Background to the Research

Part I is mainly for academic readers. Others can start at Part II.

1 Comparing Managerial Jobs and Behaviour

A comparative study of German and British managers must start by deciding how they are to be compared. While there have been studies of managerial behaviour over a period of forty years[1] there was no single model that we could adopt for making such a comparison. This made our task harder. We wanted to compare what our sample managers in the two countries were doing and how they were doing it. Unlike nearly all previous studies,[2] we also wanted to try to understand why they were doing it.

There are a number of explanations for the failure of studies over such a long period to provide us with a suitable model. The most important is that managerial behaviour, like personality, is multifaceted so that it can be described in many different ways. Four other explanations stem from the way many studies have been approached:

1. Some of the early studies concentrated on *where*, *when* and *with whom* managers were working, as well as a simple analysis of *how* they worked. They recorded the pattern of work (often using a diary method) but not its content, nor its rationale – that is, the *what* and the *why* of management work. Despite this major limitation, these studies did tell us something new about how these managers worked: that the large majority of their time was spent talking and listening, much of it with their subordinates; and that their working day was highly fragmented because they switched their attention every few minutes from one subject or person to another.

    Unfortunately, these findings were based almost exclusively on studies conducted in Sweden, Britain and America. Quite a different picture might have emerged had other countries been studied, as indicated by a small study of Japanese and Korean managers which found much less fragmentation.[3] As for the work patterns of German managers, very little is known. After a late 1940s study by W. H.,[4] nearly four decades elapsed before German researchers showed further interest in what managers actually do. These more recent studies, conducted in the late 1980s, focused on the work of top managers, and favoured the methods of the 'work activity school', which analyses managers' work activities systematically.[5]

2. Many of the researchers wanted to define the nature of managerial work by generalizing across managers even if they held highly diverse jobs. In doing so, they either ignored the studies from 1964 onwards that pointed to differences,[6] or aimed for a level of abstraction that could be thought to apply to any management job.

3. The studies are difficult to compare because they use different categories for analysis.[7]

4. There is, as has been pointed out by a number of critics,[8] a lack of theoretical orientation to many of the studies. Even those that did develop theoretical frameworks to explain their work were limited to a few explanatory variables.

One of our concerns was whether any differences that we found between the British and German managers might not be explained either by the ways the particular individuals whom we studied did the jobs – Stewart's earlier research had shown how great the variation can be between managers in comparable jobs[9] – or by differences in the companies for which they worked. Had we studied different people in the same jobs might we have found that they behaved sufficiently differently to invalidate our comparison with managers in the other country? Similarly, companies have their own distinctive cultures. The companies we chose for our case studies might well differ from other companies in the same industry and this could affect both the nature of the jobs and how managers behave. However, if the differences between British and German managers' behaviour prevail in spite of differences in personalities of jobholders, in organizations or industry structure, we have every reason to assume that our concerns are groundless. Instead we found another difference to upset our intended comparisons which was, as we shall describe later, that even in carefully matched companies, it is impossible to find identical jobs.

CHOOSING THE ANALYTICAL FRAMEWORK

Since there was no single model that we could adopt for our research, we decided that we must draw upon a number of conceptual frameworks for our analysis.

The Demands, Constraints and Choices Approach

The demands, constraints and choices approach, which was developed by Stewart,[10] has proved useful in studying jobs, perceptions and behaviour. It provides a relatively abstract, but far-reaching framework within which to analyse all manner of management jobs.

'*Demands*' means what has to be done in order not to fail in the job. The expectations that demands embody may be spelled out in the UK in periodic objective setting and in a job description. In Germany a lot of companies no longer use job descriptions. They abolished this device in order to increase flexibility and to foster the managers' motivation permanently to reflect how jobs could be extended in useful ways. Since managers stay in a job longer in German companies than in British ones job descriptions can more easily be dispensed with.

Stewart's definition of 'demands' is 'what anyone in the job *has* to do' and she further specifies that 'there are many things that a manager ought to do because they are in the job description, or because his or her boss thinks them important, but "demands" are only what *must* be done.'[11]

What determines the outer boundaries of the job are the actual or perceived *constraints*. This term designates the factors, such as resources, procedures or attitudes, that limit what the jobholder can do. These may be internal or external to the organization.

Choices are the opportunities that exist in a job for one person to spend his or her time doing different work from another person in the same job. This may just mean paying more attention to some tasks than others or, more radically, it can mean doing work that another jobholder does not do. In other words, it is the opportunity not just to do work differently, but also to do different work.

Using this abstract and general description of the dimensions of managerial jobs, Stewart succeeds in identifying different kinds of demands, constraints and choices in her empirical study as shown in Table 1.1. Stewart also shows that the extent of the demands and constraints and, therefore, the possible choices of the manager vary from position to position as illustrated in Figure 1.1.

Additionally, Stewart demonstrates, as have a number of earlier studies,[12] that the manager can shape the demands and constraints of his or her position. She has also pointed out that managers in similar jobs may differ in their perception of demands, constraints and choices which will influence the choices that they make.[13]

Table 1.1   Summary of different kinds of demands, constraints and choices
in managerial jobs

DEMANDS

Overall meeting minimum criteria of performance
Doing certain kinds of work. Such work is determined by:

The extent to which personal involvement is required in the unit's work;
Who must be contacted and the difficulty of the work relationship;
Contacts' power to enforce their expectations;
Bureaucratic procedures that cannot be ignored or delegated;
Meetings that must be attended.

CONSTRAINTS

Resource limitations;
Legal and trade union constraints;
Technological limitations;
Physical location;
Organizational constraints, especially extent to which the work of the
manager's unit is defined;
Attitudes of other people to:
   Changes in the system, procedures, organization,
   pay and conditions;
   Changes in the goods or services produced;
   Work outside the unit.

CHOICES

In how the work is done
In what work is done
Choices within a defined area:
   To emphasize certain aspects of the job
   To select some tasks and to ignore or
   delegate others
Choices in boundary management
Choices to change the area of work:
   To change the unit's domain
   To develop a personal domain:
   To become an expert
   To share work, especially with colleagues
   To take part in organizational and public activities

Source: Stewart, *Choices for the Manager* (Maidenhead: McGraw-Hill, 1982;
and Englewood Cliffs: Prentice-Hall, 1982) p. 3.

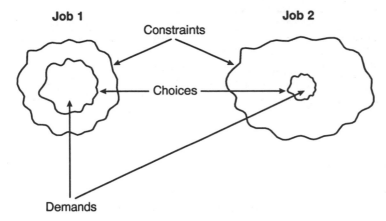

Figure 1.1 Differences in demands, constraints and choices in two jobs
(Stewart, 1991, p. 15)

A methodological problem in Stewart's work and in other studies of managerial behaviour is that there is no systematic analysis of the impact of the context on individual management jobs.[14] Therefore further theoretical concepts are required.

Role Concepts

Role concepts have proved to be useful tools for analyzing behaviour in formal organizations.[15]

A role is the sum of the expected behaviours of a jobholder. This is derived from the (normative) conception of what an individual in a certain job does or should do. It is also determined by what that individual does not or should not do.

At least three kinds of role concepts can be identified: structural, functional and interactive ones.[16] Conceptually Stewart's 'demands–constraints–choices' approach to analysing managerial jobs is related to interactive role concepts.[17] But her approach to analysing managerial jobs is more limited in its scope than the Katz and Kahn role episode model,[18] or that of Graen.[19] It does not, for example, analyse the possible discrepancies between the expectations transmitted and those received. This is important in order to achieve a more objective understanding of the demands, constraints and choices of the manager. Fondas and Stewart in a later theoretical paper discuss the relationship between Stewart's model and that of Katz and Kahn (Figure 1.2) and seek to take more account of the possibilities for enacting expectations.[20]

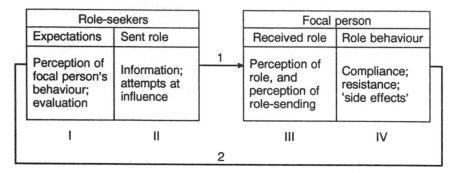

Figure 1.2 The role episode model (Daniel Katz and Robert Kahn, *The Social Psychology of Organizations*, Copyright © 1966, p. 182). (Reprinted by permission of John Wiley & Sons, Inc.)

In Katz and Kahn's role episode model, the role-senders have specific expectations which they communicate to the role-player. The jobholder, then, may or may not recognize these expectations and may or may not conform to them. Based on the actual behaviour of the role-player, the role-senders will develop new or altered role expectations. Personal, interpersonal, and organizational factors become important intervening variables in the role episode model.

Ideally, one would wish to consider the expectations of every single role-sender influencing the particular managers studied. But research efficiency dictates otherwise. The present study restricted itself to what is usually likely to be the most important role-sender, namely the manager's direct boss. The bosses of each of the middle managers were interviewed, because of their ability to influence the demands, constraints and choices of the middle managers. This helped to provide a check on the reliability of the managers' responses as well as a different perspective on what were seen as demands, constraints and choices.

It also seems important to include an analysis of organizational factors, such as the structure of the organization, the incentive and control systems, as well as specific technology used.

These organizational variables express role expectations sent to the middle managers. An awareness of these organizational factors is therefore essential in order to understand the demands and constraints on the managers in the two countries – and to establish which aspects of managerial behaviour are choice-driven.

By taking into account organizational factors and the expectations of superiors, it is possible to build up a clearer picture of each managerial position. The job under scrutiny is no longer isolated, but is seen in relation to other structural components of the organization.

But simply analysing what is expected of managers and how these expectations are perceived, does not tell us about the actual behaviour of the managers. An analysis limited to expected behaviours would not answer the *how* of managerial behaviour. To achieve this further concepts are needed.

Agendas and Networks

Kotter's study of the daily behaviour of fifteen general managers provides further important constructs for the analysis and explanation of managerial behaviour.[21] These are the concepts of 'agenda-setting', 'network-building', and 'execution'.

Agendas are mental representations of what the manager wants to do. They are concerned with the many loosely-related goals which a manager has for his or her short, middle-, or long-term responsibilities. Kotter describes the general managers as developing their agendas and spending a lot of time building *networks* of cooperative relationships with those people on whom they must depend to accomplish the tasks on their agendas – in Kotter's study this network for his general managers was probably wider than the 'role set' in the Katz and Kahn model described above. A network consists of many different people within the organization, as well as others outside it. *Execution* describes the process of implementing the agendas through the networks. The framework is useful in that it links what managers actually do with what they are trying to achieve. For example, he describes how the general managers set their agenda by asking many questions of their network. He concludes that the decision making process occurs in their minds: they can very rarely be observed making major decisions. A variety of tactics, such as humour, are used in network building. In using their network to implement their agenda they were rarely observed to give orders, rather they tried to influence others to do what they wanted.

Kotter's concepts, though distinctive and useful, only make a partial contribution to understanding managerial behaviour. There are two main limitations. First, not much attention is given to the structure of social and economic relationships, which ensure the legitimacy of rules and standards, as well as the access to certain resources, which the managers can draw upon when determining, redetermining and defending the substance of their work.[22] Kotter only considers the application of interpersonal capabilities and leaves out the institutional context of managerial actions. The pure personal–voluntary concept of managerial actions, as Kotter presents it, insufficiently portrays the actual managerial practice. Managers, too, are part of social and organizational structures which limit their actions while also facilitating them.

Second, it is doubtful how far one can generalize from the fifteen general managers whom Kotter studied to managers generally, particularly less senior managers. Managerial jobs with less-complex demands, such as those of middle managers, will have less opportunity and less need to develop their own agendas as, at least in stable situations, they may follow established problem-solving steps provided by organizational policies and procedures. Similarly they will have less scope and less need than general managers for network building.

Of course, for managers at all levels taking over new jobs, the development of agendas and networks would be important. But the time spent on these activities would diminish with experience in the job. Fulfilling the demands of the job should become routine and less time should be devoted to developing agendas and networks. Thus, the time spent in a managerial job is also likely to affect the need for agenda-setting and network-building, unless the organization is undergoing rapid change. Greater familiarity with the job will mean that the work will become more routine or script-based.[23]

GETTING DOWN TO CULTURE

Managers' Educational and Career Background

To understand further the work-behaviour of managers in different countries, it is also necessary to consider what has shaped their approaches to work: what work-related principles and rules were acquired by the jobholders prior to entering the organization and during their careers. Some of the demands on jobholders relate to their professional role. For instance, managers working in a finance role will be socialized into taking a particular approach to work, both officially, during their professional training, and unofficially, by fellow-professionals in the workplace. If qualification systems[24] and career patterns[25] differ between two countries, as they do between Britain and Germany, it can be assumed that the principles which guide managers in the two countries will also differ – as will the managers' ensuing actions and behaviour.

It is also likely that cultural differences relating to social institutions and beliefs, which are reflected in organizational principles, will manifest themselves in different understandings of management. These differences in the understanding or conception of management would naturally influence managers' actions. These conceptions of management could be considered subjective, or 'naive' theories.

These 'naive' theories are relatively long-lasting cognitive systems developed by the everyday person (*Alltagsmenschen*), based on accumulated knowledge and subjective theoretical convictions.[26] The concept of subjective theories is used to help to explain human actions, without trying to suggest they provide comprehensive explanations. For example, the general managers observed by Kotter could be said to work according to the subjective leadership theory that the successful execution of their agendas depends upon building good contacts with their colleagues, employees and superiors. Where appropriate, these subjective theories will be highlighted in our explanations.

The Broader Cultural Backcloth

The managers' educational and career background are but two contributors to the managers' behavioural make-up. There is also the broader cultural backcloth. A comparative study of managerial behaviour must recognize that individual behaviour is shaped by national culture. To this end, we shall draw upon cross-cultural studies in seeking to explain differences in behaviour. These cultural differences are reflected in national institutions – such as legal and educational institutions, employers–trades-union relationships, and prevailing organizational designs[27] – and these, in turn, will reinforce particular values and guide managerial actions.

All these cultural factors were regarded as potential influences on how the managers saw their roles and what was expected of them, and the importance they attached to network-building, as well as their perception of demands, constraints and choices.

2 Designing the Study

Management research is conventionally presented as an orderly, coherent and logical process. The research design follows on neatly from the aims, rationale and theoretical perspective of the investigation. The reality is somewhat different, particularly when the subject is complex. Limits on time, available manpower and the goodwill of informants means that some of the noble research objectives are inevitably compromised. This is especially true of cross-cultural research where the practical problems of comparison are manifold – and rendered all the more 'challenging' in the present study by the lack of indigenous German research on management work.

Our intention was to try to relate managerial work and behaviour to its cultural, sectoral and organizational setting as well as to the respective industry in which the organizations operate. To try to grasp the connections between these factors, it was important to examine the jobs of middle managers in relation to the organization as a whole. The organization imposes constraints on the choices an individual manager may take and, to a large extent, structures the demands of the job. The organizational setting, however, does not constitute an 'objective' reality, independent of the 'subjective' interpretations of individuals within it. Organizational structure does not define the jobs completely. Therefore the expectations of the bosses have to be taken into account, as a major, and often the major, individual influence on what is expected of the jobholder.

Yet the organization, both in terms of its structure and its workings, cannot be understood in isolation. It is also necessary to consider the wider context. Organizations operate within particular sectors. Therefore, certain recurring patterns of behaviour were expected to emerge among the managers based on the character of the product, the nature of the market and so on.

Beyond the boundaries of the sector, there are other sociopolitical forces at play. Such factors as the health of the national economy, the nature of financial markets (the attitude to, and the ease of, acquisition) or the export-orientation of the country will also affect the way organizations are set up and run.

There is also the cultural context to consider. To some extent this is reflected in the country's institutions: the system of qualifications, of industrial relations and of legislation. Intermingled with these institutional considerations, are the values and beliefs shared by the individuals in that culture. These value systems can be regarded as 'mental programmes'.[1]

The national culture and institutions, the peculiarities of the sector and the organization, represent a cocktail of interrelated influences which affect the way middle managers go about their jobs. Our intention was to seek to distil that mixture into its constituent elements and to try to identify which element gave rise to which kind of managerial behaviour or attitude. Obviously we could only hope at best for partial success in doing this.

The study, then, fell into three stages:

1. to establish the demands, constraints and choices of middle managers in different organizations in the two countries;
2. to compare the nature of middle management work and behaviour (as against top management work) in the two countries;
3. to try to account for the differences between the British and German middle managers.

In order to cope with the complex interdependence between context, organization and individual job, the case-study approach was deemed the most appropriate. It enables the researcher to go deeper in complex matters, which are not wholly understood, thus helping to explore the field and to assist in generating hypotheses – all the more necessary given the paucity of existing German material on the nature of managerial jobs and behaviour.

Of course, the case-study approach is labour-intensive, as well as making fairly heavy demands on the goodwill of the managers and the interpersonal sensitivity of the researchers. Yet it was considered the only approach that would do justice to the complexity and uncertainty of the research area.

The main problem faced, given agreement on the case-study method, was to assemble two populations of managers which were matched and which could be said to be representative of middle management as a layer, in their respective countries. As a preliminary to this, we had to establish the nature and size of our prospective sample and to work out what sort of dimensions we were trying to compare.

To try to give the sample a representative quality, it was considered important to select managerial jobs in different functions as well as diverse industries – the more heterogeneous the better. If this cross-section of jobs gave rise to *consistent* differences between the two countries, it would be possible to assert, with some confidence, that these constituted institutionally or culturally driven differences – rather than merely representing differences between the selected individuals, organizations or sectors.

CHOICE OF INDUSTRIES

Four considerations informed our choice of industries:

1. the industries selected had to be of roughly the same size within the national economy.
2. the industries had to be comparable in terms of their performance within the proper national economy – it was no use selecting a firm from the flourishing German mechanical engineering industry, to compare with one of Britain's diminished band of representatives in that sector.
3. in establishing appropriate industries we had to consider the spread of sectors. We wanted to include representatives from both the manufacturing and service sectors – primarily because of the obsession of previous studies with manufacturing industry.[2] Would some of those previous findings hold true for managers in service firms? Our initial desire to include an organization from the public sector was considered inappropriate, on reflection, because of the ongoing upheaval in that sector in Britain.
4. the firms selected should not be foreign-owned. This condition was intended to rule out the possibility of organizational structure or managerial behaviour being influenced by the nature of the parent-company.

While fairly broad, these four conditions were not so easy to fulfil. The problem was not one of thinking up suitable sectors, so much as gaining the required access to those companies. Both research teams had useful *entrées* to companies, but few in matching sectors – or else the access granted was uneven. For instance, the German team gained full access to a retailing company, but the British team was only able to negotiate partial access – largely because the recession was in full swing at the time. The upshot was that the retail sector had to be dropped.

Thus, the goodwill of the companies approached was another factor in our selection of sectors. We settled on the following 'choice' of industries:

1. *The brewing industry*, as a representative of manufacturing industry, produces a simple and identifiable product in both countries, as well as applying *process production* systems as its core technology.[3] The industries are of about the same size in each country but the nature of their respective markets does differ to some extent.[4]

2. *The insurance industry*, as a representative of the service sector, applies a form of *mass production* system as its core technology. This might seem strange for a service firm, but the operations performed are akin to those in mass manufacture. The insurance contracts are highly standardized which means that the administrative procedures are also highly automated: from checking applications to underwriting them, from altering or surrendering contracts to checking claims. The particular aspect of insurance on which we focused was life assurance – both the selected companies feature among the top twelve in their sectors. As with brewing, there are certain national differences in the nature of the market and in terms of regulation.

3. *The construction industry*, as another representative of the manufacturing sector, but with quite different characteristics from the brewing industry. The construction industry is project-driven, and therefore applies a *unit production* system of technology on a 'one-off' basis. The nature of the markets also differs in this sector. Again, we chose companies which operate in the same market segments and which feature among the country's top ten construction companies.

Both research teams had high-level introductions to suitable organizations in each of the three industries. It was therefore possible to discuss the project informally either with a 'facilitator' before approaching the company or with a top manager. The facilitator paved the way for this meeting by making sure that both parties knew roughly what to expect: the level of access required by the researchers, the amount of disruption it would cause to the company, and the tangible benefits to the company.

CHOICE OF JOBS

Since we wanted to gain an overall impression of middle-management behaviour in each company, it was necessary to select managers in varied functions. We opted to study managerial jobs in each of three core functions: technical, commercial, and administrative/finance.

It was agreed that we should study ten middle-management jobs in each organization. First, organizational charts were obtained for the British companies and the German insurance company. Because the German brewery had no organization chart and the construction company had only one which was restricted to the higher management levels these organizations charts had to be reconstructed by the research team. These were exchanged and we tried to find ten pairs of matched jobs for each sector. Over the whole study, this added up to thirty middle managers for each country.

In practice, finding matched jobs proved very difficult. Even positions with similar job-titles often turned out to cover quite different tasks and functions, as well as different levels of responsibility. It became clear that the allocation of tasks to jobs was, in itself, the result of different organizational principles – which stemmed from cultural and institutional differences.

The problem facing the researchers can be illustrated thus: if four labourers are building a house, they can broadly organize themselves in two ways. In one they could all have similar jobs, with each one building one side of the house. In the other, they could all have specialized roles: one digging the foundation, one mixing the cement, one laying the bricks and one putting in the window-frames. The latter system has more interdependency and requires more coordination – so it would be impossible to comment on the behaviour of those labourers without taking into account the way their work was organized. Comparing the methods of organization by looking at paired jobs is meaningless. The two sets of jobs have to be compared as systems.

To overcome this problem in our own study, it was therefore necessary to consider the organization as a whole: to look more closely at the way that responsibilities were broken down among the middle managers, and to try to understand the nature of the interdependence between the managers. For instance, it would be no use asserting that one set of managers is more network-oriented than its counterparts, if that is primarily a function of the way their work is organized.

Another input into our understanding of the middle managers and their jobs was provided by their immediate bosses. The boss's expectations of the middle manager are important in shaping the job. For most middle managers, the immediate boss probably represents the dominant 'role-sender'. This involved four to five extra interviews in each case study.

SAMPLE OF CASES

This section presents the key features that we considered relevant for an understanding of managerial jobs and behaviour for each organization studied, industry by industry.

1. Breweries

The British brewery of our study is a wholly-owned subsidiary – one among several breweries – of one of the six large companies in this country. It does not have control of sales, which is the responsibility of the parent organization. The quantities of the four sorts of beer which are produced in this brewery are determined by a department in the parent-organization on the basis of a long-term production plan.

The four sorts of beer were distributed in barrels. The brewery produced about three-quarters of a million barrels, which is about 1.23 million hectolitres of beer, in the year 1991 – which is less than half the volume of the German brewery. Turnover was £40.9 million. It had 755 employees, 179 of them in Production Departments, 86 in Engineering Services, 428 in Distribution, 24 in Finance Department, 34 in Personnel and 4 others.

Five functional managers – Personnel, Engineering Services, Distribution, Finance, and Production – reported directly to a managing director. The organization chart of the British brewery is shown in Figure 2.1.

It was a general policy in the group of the British brewery that individuals be given job objectives (Areas of Competence) by their superiors. Ideally there should be a cascade effect in that the AOCs (Areas of Competence) agreed between the Managing Director and the functional directors are then reflected in the AOCs agreed between the functional director and his/her direct reports, and so on down the line. The AOCs reflected particular priorities on the key tasks, for example, the key task for the personnel manager might be to advise managers throughout the company on personnel policy. The AOCs related to that key task would change from year to year as shaped by the business environment or strategic initiatives – so for the personnel manager it might specify revising a handbook or revising recruitment policy. The merit system took account of whether individuals achieved some or all, or surpassed, their AOCs. Some AOCs are amended through the year because of external factors which fall outside the jobholder's control – staff may be lost

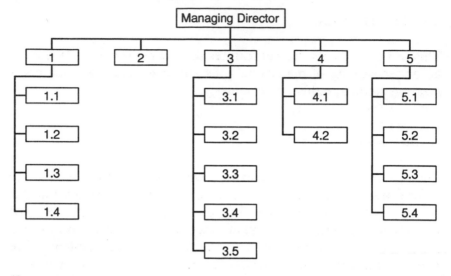

Key:

Managing Director

1   Personnel Director

　　1.1   Chief Security Officer
　　1.2   Personnel Manager
　　1.3   Fire, Health & Safety Manager
　　1.4   Training Manager

2   Engineering Services Director

3   Distribution Director

　　3.1   Distribution Operations Manager
　　3.2   Distribution Development
　　　　 Manager

　　3.3   Fleet Engineer
　　3.4   Redhill Manager
　　3.5   Distribution Manager (West)

4   Finance Director

　　4.1   Payroll Manager
　　4.2   Finance & Administration
　　　　 Manager

5   Production Director

　　5.1   Brewing & Fermenting Manager
　　5.2   Keg Plant Manager
　　5.3   Quality Systems Manager
　　5.4   Technical Manager

Figure 2.1　British brewery organization chart

and not replaced which makes the achievement of the AOC more difficult. There are reviews four times a year in which individuals can put forward the case for revising their AOCs. There is no official quota system on the number of As, Bs and Cs handed out. The trend, however, is that a handful of people – in recent years this has ranged between none and six – win A merits – which bring a bonus of 3.5 per cent. The rest are usually evenly split between Bs and Cs. An A is an outstanding achievement, B is good, C is meant to be the norm.

　　Budget proposals are prepared by the departmental managers and ratified or moderated by the Management Committee. Once the budget is agreed and approved it is fixed for the year. If something major happens which exceeds the budget then the finance function will 'trend' to the year and any savings or extra costs they know will be incurred (for budget excesses over £100 000). In normal circumstances managers are expected to stick to their budgets. And they are expected officially not to shift between headings. In practice, however, managers can make a case for setting off a deliberate saving in one category against overspending in another. Each cost centre has an expenditure control statement for each period. This is sent to both the departmental manager and immediate boss (functional director).

Every manager in the British brewery has a job description.

The British brewery is 100 per cent unionized. On the site we studied, several unions are represented, the most important of which are the Transport and General Workers Union (TGWU), General Municipal and Boilermakers Union and Amalgamated Engineering Union (AEU) (mechanical craftsmen). Before recent legislation, our British brewery operated a closed-shop policy, but not all members are active. All negotiations are local which means that middle managers in line jobs spent time in negotiations with the TGWU.

The German brewery ranks among the first five in the country. 70 per cent of its shares are owned by a large holding company, which is active in food and other industries. The rest of the shares are owned by various companies and people with no particular influence on company policies. The holding group, however, is also owner of a majority of shares in other big breweries operating in other regions of Germany.

The German brewery is only controlled by its operating results. Besides that, it is a totally independent company. It is primarily through membership in the advisory board of executives that the parent-company can influence policies.

There are, however, close links between the personnel department of this brewery and the training department of the parent-company which performs the bulk of management training for the brewery. There are also close links to the computer centre of the parent-company which provides a number of services for the subsidiaries. These links may be regarded as a form of indirect control. In the first place this is because the management training is likely to produce a preferred style of management and of management methods over all the companies. In the second place the provision of computer services, such as common software programmes, lead to common procedures in accounting and elsewhere which facilitate control by the holding company.

More important for some of the jobs studied is the relation of the German brewery to its subsidiary brewing and beverage companies. Not only are there financial control procedures but also quite a number of personal links. Some (middle) managers are also managers or even executives of the subsidiary companies as well: one of the sales managers studied, for instance, is at the same time managing executive of a subsidiary company. In this way, these subsidiaries also work as a means of personnel promotion. The German brewery also does the accounts of its subsidiaries, so the accounting department has direct links to all of them.

The German brewery concentrates on special beers (e.g. alcohol-free beer). About 70 per cent of the beer produced is packaged in bottles and sold to tied pubs, wholesalers, and supermarket chains. Sales of barrels are only regional and of marginal importance. The brewery also produces and sells mineral water.

The output of beer in 1988 was 2.9 million hectolitres (the company does not, as a rule, publish figures on its output). 69 per cent of this quantity consisted of speciality beers. The company employed 1068 people in 1987. This figure declined to 979 in 1989, and in 1990 there were only 966 people employed, 544 in the sales function, 325 in production-oriented jobs (including distribution), 93 in administrative jobs and four top managers.

The German brewery is organized by functions from the very top, i.e., from the board of executives, downward. Each of the four functions – Technology (production and related functions); Controlling and Personnel, Sales, and Finance – is represented by a member on the board of executives. These executives run their own functions relatively independently within the commonly agreed policy. One of the four members of the board of executives (Controlling and Personnel) is the managing director of the brewery. He (they were all men), however, is more like a '*primus inter pares*' within the board than a boss of the other executives. Making a team responsible for running a company is typical in Germany. Although there is no official organization chart, it is possible to describe the organization structure of the company with regard to the jobs studied as shown in Figure 2.2.

There is a difference in structure between sales and the other functions. The sales function has only three hierarchical levels so as to provide more flexibility. All other functions have at least four hierarchical levels with production having five. The five can be explained by the large span of control that would have to be handled by a manager if there were no supervisors beneath him.

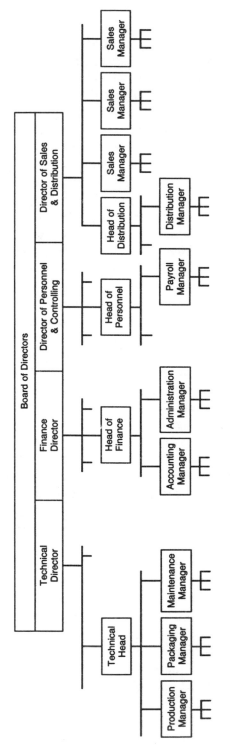

Figure 2.2 German brewery organization chart

The German brewery did away with job descriptions and official organization charts some years ago in order to allow flexibility both for the company and staff. It was also found that job descriptions were impeding 'intrapreneurship' which the company wanted to foster. The rationale of this policy was that 'obstacles to flexibility' should be abolished to allow more flexibility in reacting to market demands. One of the objectives already reached in the sales department was to have fewer hierarchical levels and thus a faster implementation of company targets set by the board of executives.

The company's control system is based on profit margins, i.e. revenues exceeding the variable costs. The production department is controlled by the amount of beer produced and packaged, by the flexibility in reacting to changes in production plans and by its costs.

Departments are controlled by budgets that include personnel costs, overheads, and machinery. Except for the sales managers, however, it is one level above the managers studied that budgets are controlled. The middle managers studied do not perceive themselves to be controlled by budgets and their bosses' interviews provide evidence that this perception is correct. Budgets are planned in detail for one year with a scope of three years. They are, however, not regarded as an iron law. If managers exceed their budgets for reasons within the company's objectives there are no adverse consequences for them. Nor are there direct consequences in terms of a bonus if they keep below their budget.

Because of the rapid growth of the German brewery in recent years there is at present no formal system to assess managers' effectiveness. In principle – except for the sales managers – it is the output in quantitative and qualitative terms which is regarded as crucial. In the production departments the budget is to gear the managers towards a cost-orientated thinking. Apart from that the budgets are relatively flexible because of other measurements of effectiveness. In no other departments is there direct impact of the budgets on control of the managers. Unlike the other managers studied the sales managers' budgets include salaries, overheads and expenses to host important customers, etc. Their subordinates also have a budget for expenses, which they control themselves. There is, however, a control of these budgets by the manager in the regular feedback talks.

The salary is not related to middle managers' performance. Nevertheless, there are job-related amendments to the salary guaranteed by the collective bargaining contract which make it possible for the company to pay their managers more than the collective agreement says. In addition there is the opportunity for the middle managers' bosses to pay them extra bonuses if they are extraordinarily pleased with their performance. This, however, can only be done after having consulted the executive board and reached agreement. In good years the company pays an annual lump sum to every employee. In 1990 this was DM 500 in cash with the company taking over the taxes.

In the German brewery union density as a whole is low. It is only in the production and distribution area where unions are – or rather the work council is – a factor to be considered.

Table 2.1 overleaf gives a more detailed breakdown of the jobs studied in the British and German breweries.

2. Insurance Companies

When pensions are included, the British insurance company which we studied belongs to the top three in this particular industry. However, the UK life assurance industry is very fragmented with no company having more than a 10 per cent share of the total market.

In 1990 the company had about £15 billion insurance liabilities, provisions and reserves, £3 billion of which concerned life assurances. The total number employed in the British life assurance company in 1990 was approximately 3500 plus a self-employed sales force of 2500–3000 which is tied to the company.

The British company offers pensions and life assurance, and within life assurance savings plans (death), mortgage plans (death), protection plans (personal risk) and many older-type policies.

Figure 2.3 shows the organizational chart for the British company. Details are only given for the customer services department which deals with conventional life assurances.

In the British company every manager has a job description which is considered an integral part of the grading structure and of the managers' appraisal system. It includes 'principal accountabilities' which are included in the annual senior management review and which form a basis for the objective-setting. So every year there is an automatic review of job descriptions because principal accountabilities must genuinely reflect the job. They are also used as a basis for recruitment.

Each department head is responsible for submitting an annual budget. Constraints are laid down centrally which limit what managers can ask for – but everyone has to go through a negotiating process every year. The budget includes staff salaries and share of computer services, but no contribution to overheads.

Table 2.1   Brewing industry

Jobs selected in British company	Jobs selected in German company
Brewing and Fermenting Manager	Production Manager (*Leiter Produktion*)
Keg Plant Manager	Packaging Manager (*Leiter Flaschenabfüllung*)
Technical Manager	Maintenance Manager (*Leiter Instandhaltung*)
Distribution Manager	Distribution Manager (*Regionalleiter Logistik*)
Administration and Finance Manager	Accounting Manager (*Leiter Finanzbuchhaltung*)
Payroll Manager	Payroll Manager (*Leiter Entgeltbüro*)
Retail Warehouse Manager	Administration Manager (*Leiter Kundenbuchhaltung*)
Depot Manager	3 Sales Managers (*3 Verkaufsbereichsleiter*)
Shift Manager Training Manager	

Boss interviews	
Production Director	Head of Technik (*Betriebsleiter Technik*)
Distribution Director	Head of Distribution (*Distributionsleiter*)
Finance Director	Head of Finance (*Leiter Hauptabteilung Finanzen*)
Personnel Director	Director of Sales (*Vorstand Absatz*)

Annual objectives are set in agreement with the immediate boss. They consist of between seven and ten measures against which the manager will be judged at the end of the year. The objectives are supposed to be reviewed and refocused at monthly meetings – but not all the bosses find time for these monthly discussions.

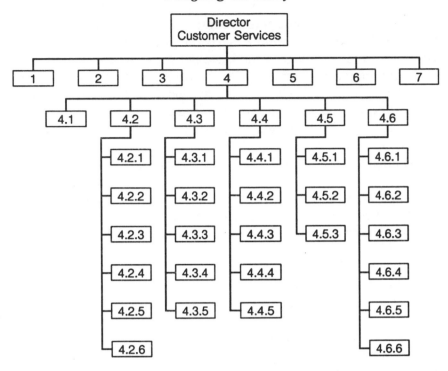

Key:

Director Customer Services

1   Individual Pensions Manager

2   Unit Assurance Manager

3   Group Pensions Manager

4   Conventional Life Manager

    4.1   Senior Underwriting Manager

    4.2   Existing Business Manager
        4.2.2   Technical Support Manager
        4.2.3   Evening Workforce Manager
        4.2.4   Alterations Manager
        4.2.5   Agency Surrenders Manager

    4.3   Quality Control Manager
        4.3.1   Quality Assurance Manager
        4.3.2   Help Desk Manager
        4.3.3   Quality Facilitator
        4.3.4   System Coordination Manager
        4.3.5   Training Manager

    4.4   New Business Manager
        4.4.1   Agency New Business Manager

        4.4.2   Technical Support Manager
        4.4.3   Evening Workforce Manager
        4.4.4   Underwriting Manager
        4.4.5   Consultancy New Business Manager

    4.5   Technical Services Manager
        4.5.1   Death Claims Manager
        4.5.2   Maturities Manager
        4.5.3   Scheme Business Manager

    4.6   Renewals Manager
        4.6.1   Agency Renewals Manager
        4.6.2   Deputy Agency Renewals Manager
        4.6.3   Consultancy Renewals Manager
        4.6.4   PGA Manager
        4.6.5   Renewals Technical Consultants
        4.6.6   Evening Workforce Manager

5   Business Requirements Manager

6   Finance Manager

7   Resources Manager

Figure 2.3   British insurance company organization chart

There is usually a financial element in the objectives (e.g. operating within budgetary constraints); a quality of service element (e.g. reducing errors, complaints, turn-around time, or uncertified sickness); a productivity element (e.g. increase productivity by 5 per cent). In addition, there are often specific task objectives such as introducing procedure manuals. There may also be an intangible objective to do with improving morale, joining the quality initiative, or motivating and developing staff.

It is intended that there should be a cascade effect with objectives interlocking with those above and below. So the process is that the individual talks to subordinates and then submits suggested objectives to the boss. The boss reviews these and feeds in objectives which he or she has been set and these can then be agreed between boss and manager.

The German life assurance company ranked between 10th and 15th place, in the 1990's ranking of insurance companies, in posted premiums and in stock of assurances. On both measures the company improved its position in relation to its competitors. It only offers life assurances (savings and protection plans).

The German life assurance company is controlled by its operating results only. Apart from that it is a totally independent company. It is only on its advisory board that the major shareholders have an influence on policies and, particularly, on recruiting the members of its board of directors.

In 1990 the German life assurance company administered 1.4 million contracts. It had 1976 employees in 1990, 955 of them in the sales force, organized in 66 district offices. 1021 employees worked in the central office.

Figure 2.4 shows parts of the organization chart for the German company. It also has a board of executives whose members are responsible for different functions and/or businesses: Subsidiaries, Contracts, Customer Services, Sales Force, General Administration (personnel, planning, etc.). These executives head the respective departments and collectively they are responsible for the general policy of the company.

The structure of the German company underwent a drastic change during the past few years. Information systems were implemented in order to facilitate structural change. A functional grouping within the customer services department was replaced by grouping by customers. Each department now performs all necessary operations for a certain number of customers. By 1992 (after we had completed our study) the New Business department was also integrated into the

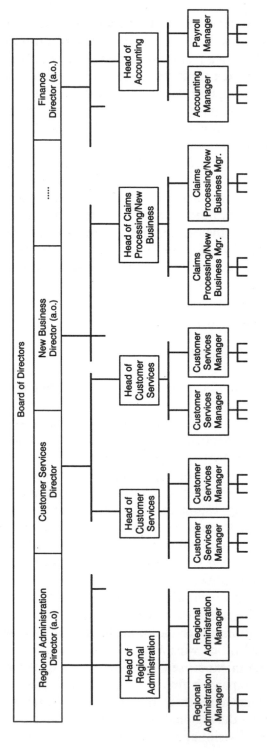

Figure 2.4 German insurance company organization chart

customer services department. There are two main reasons for this integration. The first is to improve quality of customer service by providing a full service from one department, and, within a department, by making each clerk responsible for a number of customers. For these customers he or she provides all services such as checking new contracts or changing contractual terms. The second reason for the integration is to motivate the clerks by giving them more varied tasks and thereby a more interesting job.

The salary is not related to middle managers' performance. The payment system of middle managers follows the collective bargaining contract within that industry. The middle managers are paid monthly: they earn a guaranteed sum per month with a minimum of 37.5 hours a week. Nevertheless, there are job related amendments to the salary guaranteed by the collective bargaining contract which makes it possible for the company to pay their managers more than the collective agreement says.

Table 2.2 opposite shows the jobs studied in the insurance companies in Britain and Germany.

3. Construction Companies

The British construction company studied is among the top five in its country by turnover.

It has five divisions for the different aspects of its business. Operations are performed in seventeen regional units which form part of eight construction regions each with a turnover of £40–50 million a year. Construction regions are fairly autonomous business units. They are responsible for marketing, and acquiring the work, as well as the planning, estimating, purchasing, and – quite critically – for the staffing of these projects. On the commercial side, they are responsible for cost control during the project and then accounting for it afterwards. Head Office involvement is restricted to advice or coordination as opposed to direct control. But projects above a certain size (tenders over £10 million in value) have to be cleared with the managing director before they are taken on by a region. Marketing is centralized for national clients, such as the retail stores; and, if a regional office wins a project of a certain complexity, it is possible to bring in expertise from other parts of the group.

The British company is first organized according to divisions and then the divisions have their regional organizations, while in the German company the regional organization structure comes first and is then further divisionalized according to the type of product.

Table 2.2 Insurance industry

Jobs selected in British company	Jobs selected in German company
Existing Business Manager	4 Customer Services Manager (4 *Büroleiter Kundenbetreuung*)
New Business Manager	2 Regional Administration Managers (2 *Büroleiter Außenorganisation*)
Renewals Manager	2 Claims Processing Managers /New Business Managers (*Büroleiter und stellvertretender Abteilungsleiter Antragsbearbeitung*)
Alterations Manager	Payroll Manager (*Büroleiter Lohn & Gehaltsabrechnung*)
Quality Assurance Manager	Accounting Manager (*Büroleiter Hauptbuchhaltung*)
Technical Services Manager Actuarial Manager Valuation Manager Senior Financial Accountant Sales Operations Manager	

Boss interviews	
Sales Director	Head of Regional Administration (*Abteilungsleiter Außenorganisation*)
Finance Director	Head of Accounting (*Abteilungsleiter Rechnungswesen*)
Actuarial Director	Head of Claims Processing/New Business (*Abteilungsleiter Antragsbearbeitung*)
Customer Services Director	2 Heads of Customer Services (2 *Abteilungsleiter Kundenbetreuung*)
Conventional Life Manager	

The regional organization in which our British study took place has its own board of management with the regional director as its chairman. Beneath the regional director, there are eight managers each heading a function: marketing, estimating, commercial, quality, administration, and so on. The size of their departments varies from one or two-man operations (quality manager, training manager), to the construction manager and the commercial manager who have around fifty subordinates each.

Each construction project has a site manager (technical) and a quantity surveyor (commercial) assigned to it. These report to separate bosses, who also have separate bosses and the two only come together at regional director level. The structure is further complicated because the heads of department are answerable to their functional directors at head office, as well as to the regional director locally.

The organizational chart is shown in Figure 2.5.

The total remuneration package of the middle managers in the British company consists of: salary, additional benefit for long service (though minimal actual differential now); plus private medical insurance and fully expensed company car (with petrol) for those over the £20 000 threshold. Only in the Homes division do sales people receive incentives. Profit-related bonuses are only paid for the top levels (heads of business units and top of the group).

All managers of the British company have job descriptions which are reviewed at least once a year by the jobholder and his or her manager. In the German company, job descriptions are not in use.

In the British company, there is a monthly review of current contracts. The figures are prepared by the site Quantity Surveyor and show anticipated profit. This is a subjective assessment and the job of the Managing Quantity Surveyor, when reporting upwards, is to indicate whether the assessment is pessimistic or optimistic.

The cost and value of construction projects is monitored weekly, monthly and quarterly, by the project manager and his superiors.

The budgets at the British company seem to mean something different from most companies. They are not a sum of money allotted which must not be exceeded, but rather a minimum target turnover which must be achieved. Thus, each region would have a budget which it has to surpass, which is really an objective the managers have to achieve.

The British company runs a job review system where bosses talk to their subordinates one-to-one on a yearly basis – to discuss how they are getting on with their work and what can be done to improve it. The job reviews are not linked to pay and there is no grading system attached. It is intended to improve working relationships and to lead to recommendations for improving performance. The idea is also to try to identify people's weak points and to try to develop those. The job description is mainly used as an *aide-mémoire* for these reviews.

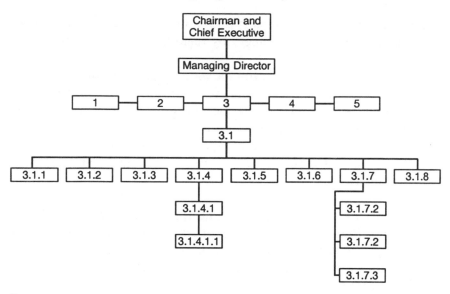

Key:

Chairman and Chief Executive

Managing Director

1   Marketing Director

2   Estimating Director

3   Divisional Director

   3.1   Regional Director
      3.1.1   Regional Planning Manager
      3.1.2   Regional Administration Manager
      3.1.3   Regional Safety Advisor
      3.1.4   Construction Manager
         3.1.4.1   Construction Manager
            3.1.4.1.1   Site Manager
      3.1.5   Regional Manager
      3.1.6   Regional Training Officer
      3.1.7   Regional Commercial Manager
         3.1.7.1   Regional Purchasing Manager
         3.1.7.2   Subcontracts/Materials Manager
         3.1.7.3   Regional Quantity Surveyor
      3.1.8   Regional Quality Manager

4   Financial Controller

5   Company Commercial Director

Figure 2.5   British construction company organization chart

The German company studied is among the top three in its industry. More than 25 per cent of the shares of the German company are owned by one of Germany's three big banks, the rest is scattered. The company is highly regionalized. There are seven regional offices, each of which is autonomous. Some regional offices are structured by product, others by regions, and in some there is a mixture of both.

The company as a whole offers a wide range of products, such as buildings, bridges, tunnels, roads. However, the regional offices may differ considerably in their production programme, depending on the specific market conditions they find in their region.

The top level of the German company is formed by a board of six executives who have functional as well as divisional and regional responsibilities:

1. Company Planning, Strategy and Coordination, Personnel, Legal Affairs, Public Relations, Insurances, Audit; one regional subsidiary (the largest one); several divisions;
2. Central Construction, Technical Offices, R&D, several regional offices; several divisions;
3. Development of Machinery; several regional offices; several divisions;
4. Eastern Europe, Great Britain; several divisions;
5. Finance, Mergers and Acquisitions, Central Services; several regional offices;
6. Accounting, Taxes, Controlling, Purchasing, Investment Planning; several regional offices; several divisions.

On the second level we find the regional offices. Each regional subsidiary has regional offices and/or divisions like Surface Workings, Underground Workings, Industrial Customers, etc.

The regional offices as well as the offices of subregions are headed by two executives, one technical and one commercial. They are supposed to form a team. This structure was chosen in order to give equal weight to technical and commercial considerations in top-level decisions of regional offices. The organization chart of the regional office in which the study took place is shown in Figure 2.6.

The German company has a profit-sharing system for managers from the level of site managers upwards. The bonuses which are dependent on the profits achieved in individual projects can reach impressive sums.

In the regional offices of the German company weekly meetings are scheduled in which the project manager, the technical and commercial branch managers of the subregions and the head of commercial control check and discuss progress of projects on the basis of computer printouts.

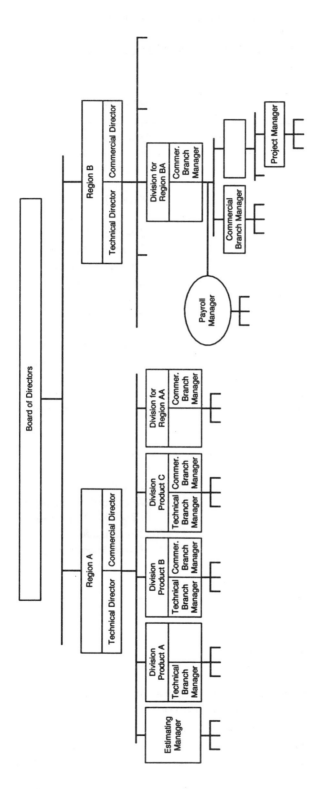

Figure 2.6 German construction company organization chart

The jobs studied in the British and German construction companies are given in Table 2.3.

Table 2.3   Construction industry

Jobs selected in British company	Jobs selected in German company
2 Contracts Managers	5 Commercial Branch Managers (5 *kaufmännische Zweigniederlassungsleiter*)
2 Managing Quant. Surveyors	2 Technical Branch Managers (2 *technische Zweigniederlassungsleiter*)
2 Purchasing Managers	Project Manager (*Oberbauleiter*)
Marketing Manager	Payroll Manager (*Abteilungsleiter Lohnbüro*)
Estimating Manager	Estimating Manager (*Leiter Kalkulation und Arbeitsvorbereitung*)
Quality Manager Training Manager	

Boss interviews	
Regional Director	2 Commercial Directors (2 *kaufmännische Hauptniederlassungsleiter*)
Regional Commercial Manager	2 Technical Directors (2 *technische Hauptniederlassungsleiter*)
Regional Construction Manager Regional Administration Manager	

RESEARCH METHOD

The aim of this study was to establish detailed empirical evidence on what managers do in the two countries, which would make it possible to address complex theoretical issues.

While aiming to make the study as representative as possible of middle management in the two countries, the size of the sample (60 middle managers and 26 bosses) is not statistically meaningful. From the British point of view, this need not present a problem since the research fits into a wider body of related literature on managerial work.[5] In Germany, however, there is insufficient existing material on the actual work of managers. Research to date, in Germany, has followed one of two directions: either being conceptual in nature, taking up prescriptive issues in management rather than looking empirically into what managers really do;[6] or else, trying to replicate Mintzberg's findings for Germany.[7] In the German context, we were therefore working nearly from scratch, and trying to establish a core of raw material from which to make comparisons.

Another problem with the existing body of literature applies to both countries. It is the assumption, often implicit, that managerial work and behaviour are independent of culture. Trying to identify whether there was such a thing as a British model of management as distinct from a German one, meant generating hypotheses rather than testing them. This was intended as an exploratory study whose findings might be confirmed, qualified or rejected by subsequent survey research.

The problem with case-study research (semi-structured interviews, analysis of documents and observation), as compared with survey studies, is that the coverage of respondents is narrower and that the analysis of results is slower and more complex. On the other hand, there are particular problems associated with the survey approach which made it unsuitable for the purpose of our research. The first problem has to do with the multiple-choice questionnaires typically used in previous cross-cultural comparisons. Child and Loveridge point out three specific problems:

(a) A strong prior conceptualization of research issues and variables drawing on existing theories, (b) a 'structured operationalization' of these variables, and (c) analysis through the interpretation of differences in mean scores allocated to variables according to a predetermined set of categories.[8]

Although studies of this type have revealed similarities and differences across cultures, there is still the problem of finding linguistic equivalents when labelling issues. This difficulty cannot be solved by careful back-and-forth translation, since culture-specific thinking makes it extremely difficult to create identical scale intervals in different languages.[9]

A further problem in using the survey method for cross-cultural research lies in the conceptual ethnocentrism of the measures,[10] which are hardly suitable for capturing qualitative values. Cross-cultural research therefore has to be careful not to introduce culture as an independent variable on an *ex-post* basis, i.e. to introduce culture as a factor to explain differences after the study had been conducted.

Having settled on the case-study approach, some problems still had to be solved. We had agreed to use a semi-structured questionnaire for the interviews. The questionnaire was designed jointly by both research teams in lengthy discussion, so as to make sure that the questions probed the same issues in both countries. Initially designed in English, the questionnaire was translated into German by the German team, who then got an independent translator to put it back into English. This version of the questionnaire was reviewed with the British research team, then piloted in both countries.

The pre-test phase involved about ten managers from assorted industries in each country. These trial interviews gave the researchers a feel for the length of the interview, the need to probe certain areas and the extent to which interviewees could be allowed to digress or expand on answers. On this evidence, the interview schedule was further modified during joint discussion. In producing the final version of the interview schedule, we were careful to ensure not only that we covered the same issues, but also that we agreed on the relevant prompts to be used with particular questions.

While interviews provide some insight into the manager's job and conduct, the answers are filtered by the respondent's consciousness. Managers may be tempted to give answers which present them in the best light or which they think the researcher wants to hear. Management work is too easily rationalized and sanitized in retrospective accounts, diary records, and especially interviews.

This problem can be counteracted by supplementing interviews with observation research. Using this approach, it is the researcher who does the interpreting. Observation research also has the merit of yielding unsuspected insights. It raises issues which the researcher would not have considered covering, and provides actual examples which the respondent would not have dreamt of supplying.

The criticism sometimes levelled at observation is that the managers can change their performance to suit the audience. This argument ignores the reality of management work which is both unprogrammable and highly interactive.[11] This means, first, that managers have to react to events and to take on-the-spot decisions; and second, that the possibility of managers acting differently is constrained by the expectations of their role set.

The main problem associated with cross-cultural comparisons is the likelihood of cultural bias or cultural blinkers (ethnocentricity).

Sharing many of the same values as the managers s/he observed, the 'host' researcher may be oblivious to the distinctiveness of certain attitudes or types of behaviour. It was in an attempt to remove this distortion that we came up with the idea of joint-observation with two or three managers in each firm.

The joint-observation process raises two further practical problems: first, it means that the researchers have to be sufficiently fluent in the other language to get the gist of what is going on; and second, it requires sensitivity on the part of the researchers to the circumstances – depending on the size of the office, nature of contacts, irritability of the manager being observed. As a result, the joint-observation process evolved with the research: it started with two people shadowing the same manager simultaneously; then we tried watching the same person on consecutive days; and finally, we settled on partial joint-observation – that is, joint-observation in the manager's office, but only one researcher following the manager around the company, so as to minimize the problem of inhibiting informal exchanges.

An important advantage of joint-observation is that it gives the researchers a chance to reconcile differences in approach or outlook. It also provides an opportunity to explore ideas while impressions are still fresh; allowing the researchers to discuss emerging idiosyncrasies *in situ*, thus pointing the home researcher's attention to them or correcting the foreign researcher's false impressions. Furthermore, irrespective of whether or not the 'guest' researcher formulates any original ideas while abroad, having seen 'what it is like' provides the essential context for understanding, questioning and interpreting the transcripts and findings of the other team.

Joint-observation, then, effectively neutralized the problem of ethnocentricity at the fieldwork stage. To counter the same problem at the later analysis stage, the interpretation of findings was organized as an on-going iterative process between the two research teams. A 'summit' meeting was held every six months, with the researchers engaged in the fieldwork meeting more frequently throughout the project to deal with specific features in the analysis of cases.

Research Procedure

To collect the necessary information about the managers in Britain and Germany, a number of methods and instruments were used (these are summarized in Table 2.4).

Table 2.4 Summary of methods used to collect information

Method	Information targeted
Library search	Background information on industry and news clippings on the company
Preliminary interview with senior manager	More detailed background information about the company and its various systems; collection of organization charts and job descriptions
Pre-interview questionnaire	Factual information about the jobs to be studied and the jobholder's background
Semi-structured interview (manager)	Designed to get a deeper understanding of the job and the manager's perception of it
Semi-structured interview (boss)	Designed to get a fuller picture of the subordinate's job: the level of choice, the boss's demands and expectations
Non-participant observation solo and joint	Provides a cross-check on the answers given in interviews, provides tangible evidence, and raises unexpected issues

The first stage involved the collection of background information on the company: starting with reading through industry profiles and newspaper cuttings on the organization; and culminating with an open-ended interview with a senior manager, at which time we gathered essential documents such as organization charts and job descriptions.

Having determined the specific jobs which were of interest, we were able to send out a three-page questionnaire to the selected managers prior to interviewing them. This questionnaire (see Appendix 1) provided us with details about previous educational and occupational background, as well as factual information concerning the present job – number of subordinates, location of boss, nature and duration of periodic meetings attended, and so on. As with the main interview schedule, this questionnaire was tested and revised before its eventual application.

Next came the semi-structured interview (see Appendix 1). The interview schedule was designed to probe the following broad areas:

1. *Tasks and responsibilities* perceived responsibilities and priorities, how the managers feel about their jobs and where they see the difficulties.

2. *Work pattern* how much time is spent doing what kinds of work and what scope there is to change that pattern.
3. *Contacts* networks and relationships; the nature of contacts vertically and horizontally, internally and externally.
4. *Understanding of management* what managers expect of others and what they feel is expected of them; what they regard as effective and ineffective management.

As mentioned earlier this questionnaire was jointly devised, then tested in each country, and revised in the light of that experience. It was eventually applied in all cases in both countries in the same way. The interviews were recorded, then transcribed for analysis.

The bosses' interview schedule (see Appendix 1) was an abridged version of the middle manager's schedule. It focused on the job of the subordinate, rather than on the boss's own job. The aim was to try to understand the framework within which the subordinate operated: level of freedom, what the boss expected, and performance measures. The interview lasted between 30 and 40 minutes as opposed to between 80 and 120 minutes for the middle managers.

The observation phase involved day-long shadowing of managers for two- or three-day periods. Half of the managers shadowed cooperated with joint-observation as described above. The recording sheet for the observation was semi-structured. The left-half of the table covered the nature and duration of the activity, while the right side was left blank (see Appendix 1). Thirteen of the thirty German managers were observed and fourteen of the British.

The purpose of the left-hand side of the sheet was to enable the researcher to record rapidly with a series of ticks what was going on: the location, what type of activity, who else was involved, whether it was over the phone or face-to-face – thus freeing time for a more detailed description (comments and reminders) to be recorded on the right-hand side.

Comparing the Case-Studies

Descriptive case-studies were produced on the basis of the information collected using the instruments described above. The fieldwork took place in 1991 and 1992. Having completed the first case-study, the research teams met to refine the categories for the analysis. This led to slight alterations for the subsequent cases. For instance, initially we asked for the full set of pre-interview questionnaires to be returned before the interviews started. Finding that some of these questionnaires had been inaccurately or inappropriately completed, we modified the procedure so that the managers completed the questionnaire in the researcher's presence, just before the interview.

The analysis also showed that the managers reacted differently to the shadowing exercise. While the British managers tended to see it as something of a game, their German counterparts took it far more seriously and sometimes seemed inhibited by observation.[12] In the light of this experience, we sometimes had to adapt our observation to the circumstances, as mentioned above.

It is worth adding though, that even distorted behaviour can be revealing. What is the nature of that distortion? Do the managers 'play to the gallery' or do they try to 'play it by the book'? As Lawrence points out:

> Not all national cultures give the same priority to 'putting on a good show' as does the British: impression management is a variable dependent, not an independent variable.[13]

There are a couple of explanations for German reticence at the prospect of observation, compared with British insouciance. First, the idea of being shadowed is not alien to British managers who may be used to having students or even schoolchildren shadowing them. David Lodge's best-selling novel, *Nice Work*, is based on the contrast between an academic and a manufacturing director who take part in a shadowing exchange scheme.

Second, from the German viewpoint, there is something rather odd about the exercise. In Britain, the idea that managers can learn from other managers in unrelated fields is well-established. In Germany, they take a rather more specific view of management: 'What on earth can a production manager in the brewing industry learn from me, an administration manager in a construction company?'

CONCLUSION

The study exposed and attempted to overcome some of the methodological drawbacks of previous cross-cultural studies. It confirmed the need to try out and modify tools in the study of management work – rather than plod on purposefully with the tools as first designed (even after being piloted). For instance, when the joint-observation proved to cause difficulties with those being observed, we came up with sequential observation. Similarly, after the first case-study, when it became apparent that some interview questions were yielding little, we changed the questionnaire. It was the questionnaire for the bosses which was most revised.

Part II

The Findings

3 Different Roads to Managerial Competence

Before looking in detail at the background, training and careers of the two populations of managers studied, some scene-setting may be helpful. What follows is a brief description of the provision of education, training and development in the two countries.

EDUCATION IN THE TWO COUNTRIES

Education Systems

Germany has a tripartite school system whereby the academically oriented will attend a *Gymnasium* while the vocationally directed will opt for *Realschule* or *Hauptschule*. The *Gymnasium* enjoys the greatest prestige, followed by the *Realschule*, with the *Hauptschule* at the bottom. Nevertheless, the last-named do not suffer from the same notoriety as did the old British secondary moderns.

In the British system, 90 per cent of secondary school pupils attend comprehensive schools. But private schools educate almost 20 per cent of all British sixth-formers (16–18), and 25 per cent of university entrants. Private schools are of little significance in Germany.

On successfully completing their secondary education, German pupils are awarded the *Abitur*. This certificate is the approximate but much broader-based equivalent of the A-level in Britain. It guarantees entry to universities and polytechnics (*Fachhochschulen*), subject to available spaces. Those who attend a technical high school will be awarded a technical *Abitur* which restricts access to technical college. The subjects on offer in a technical college are more limited than those at a general college or a university.

Advanced further education in Britain includes the Higher National Diplomas and Certificates offered by the Business and Technician Education Council (BTEC), degrees, some professional qualifications such as those of the Institute of Bankers and the accountancy bodies. Typically, access to these type of courses will require GCE A-level passes. For instance, admission to university requires at least 2 GCE A-levels. Figure 3.1 shows the general structure of publicly maintained education in the UK.

Figure 3.2 shows the basic structure of the education system in Germany.

Vocational Training

In Britain, the role of apprenticeship has little bearing on the education and training of aspiring managers. It is associated rather with the preparation of skilled craftsmen in engineering and other sectors of manufacturing. But in Germany, even some of those who have completed their *Abitur* elect to serve an apprenticeship, for example in banking, prior to studying at university, but the majority go directly to university. Each year, about 550 000 German school-leavers sign apprenticeship contracts with companies. Apprenticeship courses in Germany last two or three years depending on the subject and the prior education of the candidates. They link in-company training with specialized and general education in *Berufsschulen* (vocational schools). This is the so-called 'dual system' which is often touted as the cornerstone of Germany's business success.[1]

The practical part of the apprenticeship takes place within a training facility under the supervision of a qualified instructor. The theoretical part of the apprenticeship is given in vocational schools, where almost half of the trainees' time is devoted, not to their trade, but to classes in mathematics, German and general studies.

The dual system covers both public and private organizations. Every German profession has its own training programme and all companies employing apprentices must conform to it. The system is tightly regulated by statute, and efforts are made to keep training up-to-date while avoiding over-specialization.

Local chambers of commerce accredit instructors and organize the standardized exams which trainees must pass in order to qualify. This guarantees that qualified apprentices are of a certain calibre, a standard which corresponds to the competences and knowledge of a skilled worker or clerk.

Pre-Entry Management Education

The provision of management education at pre-entry level has flourished in Britain over the past twenty years. It is increasingly

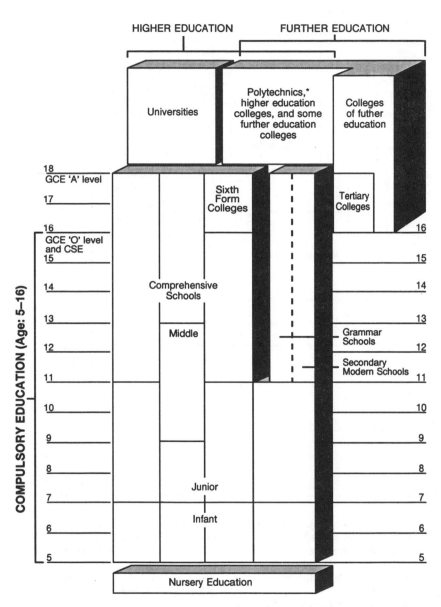

* Became universities in 1993

SOURCE: Steve Sharples and Vikki Carty, *Vocational Training in the United Kingdom* (CEDEFOP – European Centre for the Development of Vocational Training, Berlin, 1985). (Reproduced with permission.)

Figure 3.1 Publicly maintained education in the UK

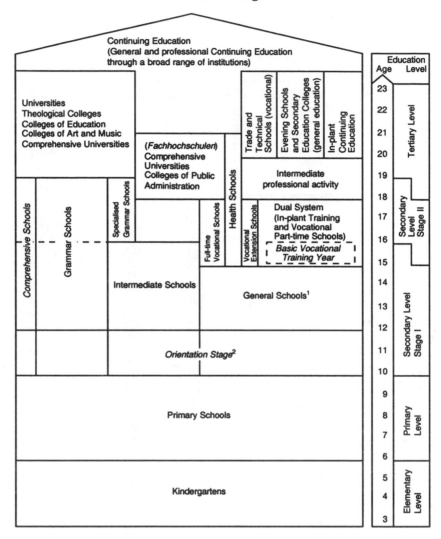

[1] About 27 per cent of pupils in General Schools in addition attended an additional tenth school year.
[2] About 72 per cent of pupils in fifth and sixth school years attended the Orientation stage.
* There are slight differences within the individual Länder

Figures in right-hand column show the earliest possible age of entry in an uninterrupted progress through the education system.
The size of the rectangles is not proportional to the numbers attending

SOURCE: Grund- und Strukfurdaten 1984/5: Der Bundesminister für Bildung und Wissenschaft.

Figure 3.2 Basic structure of the education system in Germany

possible to study business at college or university. There is a wide variety of certificates and degrees, ranging from the subdegree certificates of BTEC and the Higher National Diploma through to one-year and two-year postgraduate MBAs.

While the provision of management education is rather diffuse, the demand for it is strong, with undergraduate courses in business and management oversubscribed fourfold in the mid-1980s. Universities and educational institutions were only able to supply one-seventh of the annual replacement stock of 90 000 new management recruits in 1986 with these qualifications.

In Germany, the main subjects in order of popularity at degree level are: mechanical and production engineering; economics and *Betriebswirtschaft* (business management); and social studies.[2] In most programmes, there is a period of placement in industry or commerce.

The closest that German universities come to what Anglo-Saxons call management studies or business administration, is business management (*Betriebswirtschaftslehre*). While there is substantial overlap between the two courses, there is also an important difference. Undergraduate management courses in Britain are founded on the conviction that management is a stand-alone discipline: there is heavy emphasis on organizational behaviour, marketing and comparative management. This is in contrast with the German view of management which requires competence in several disciplines, notably economics, finance and bookkeeping. The German courses have more to do with techniques and the various business functions; while the Anglo-Saxon ones are concerned with the principles and the process of management. To characterize the difference, German graduates are educated *for* management rather than trained *in* management.[3]

Many universities in Germany today suffer from being overcrowded, and are criticized for the length of courses, which can be dispiriting for students. University courses last an average of seven years, compared with just 3.3 years in Britain. With military service included, the average male German student does not reach the job market until the age of 28 (21 in Britain).

Universities in Britain are autonomous bodies, awarding their own degrees. In Germany the Federal States are in charge of the universities, which are nevertheless self-administered bodies establishing their own regulations. However, these must be approved by the state government. In most of the subjects the students are awarded a 'Diplom', which is their first university degree.

Another noteworthy difference relating to higher education is the view of doctorates as managerial credentials. University graduates in Germany, with directorial ambitions, are well advised to take a doctorate in a relevant subject. In 1985, over 35 per cent of management board members in Germany's *Aktiengesellschaften* (AGs) (corporations) had the right to be addressed as '*Herr Doktor*'. The corresponding figure among board members of quoted AGs, was over 40 per cent; and for the 100 largest AGs, the figure topped the 50 per cent mark.[4] In Britain, the statistics are hardly worth collecting.

Professional Institutes

In much the same way as the vocational route was only relevant to the preparation of German managers, so the professional route is mainly pertinent to that of British managers. While such bodies exist in Germany, their role is primarily to organize conferences and disseminate information. Membership does not help in job applications where formal qualifications are considered to be of greater importance. Nor is membership in Germany status-enhancing, in the way that it is in Britain.

The professional approach in Britain mixes tutored work-experience with formal study. There is a graded series of qualifications in the different professional bodies corresponding to varying levels of membership, and culminating with full membership of an institution.

Foremost among the professional bodies valued in management in Britain, have been the accountancy institutions. Accountancy is a well-worn path into general management jobs throughout industry. Each year, about 10 per cent of British undergraduates seek to become qualified accountants. Britain's accountancy profession is larger and more organized than in Germany.

Besides the bodies serving the accountancy profession, other professional and accrediting institutions have also prospered in Britain. These may be attached to a particular sector, such as the Institute of Bankers or the Institute of Brewers, or they can cut across industries, such as the Institute of Marketing and the Institute of Personnel Managers.

This approach, combining experience and study, fits in well with the pragmatic tradition in Britain – even if the education dispensed was never intended to prepare individuals for a career in general management. It is not surprising, then, that one of the most-heralded initiatives designed to improve British management, was the 'Management Charter'. The idea was to establish a national qualification for chartered managers. The qualification was to be awarded on the basis of on-the-job development and experience, together with appropriate and timely inputs of formal training. Although the initiative may have lost momentum, its conception endorses British commitment to the professional approach.

While the British and German approaches to preparing managers differ in many respects, there is an interesting parallel between Germany's apprenticeship system and Britain's professional approach. The fact that both involve formal education and training in the workplace, makes one look like a delayed version of the other. This consistency reflects a practical bias in both cultures.

Training and Development

Large companies in Germany conduct most of their *Weiterbildung* (management development) programmes internally, making full use of their extensive short-course facilities. A strong commitment to training and development, is allied to a firm belief that the best programmes are company-specific. The management development is dispensed by company trainers, senior managers or bought-in specialists from universities or polytechnics.[5] Typically, the lower the managerial rank, the greater the development received.

For medium-sized companies, the costs of internal training can be onerous, and there is more likely to be recourse to external courses. The programmes run by the Chambers of Industry and Commerce feature heavily in the provision of training and development.

British companies also tend to regard in-house or specially tailored courses, including MBAs, as being more relevant to their needs. In contrast, the preference of British managers, who have greater job-mobility than their German counterparts, is for formal external qualifications that enhance transferability and attractiveness to other employers. This promotes a certain tension between employers and managers to which allusion was made in two major studies, the Handy report,[6] and the Constable–McCormick report.[7]

In comparing how the two countries 'grow' their managers, it is far easier to discern a consistent pattern in the German model of education, training and development. The British model seems to offer a wider number of routes into management posts but no dominant philosophy of how management can best be learnt, taught or developed.

COMPARING OUR SAMPLE

Educational Credentials

While the sample-size is too small to establish significant differences, and was limited to three industries, the managers in our study did reflect some of the national peculiarities and emphases highlighted above. The two key differences between the British and German managers were:

1. the completion of an apprenticeship by the German middle managers;
2. the widespread membership of a professional body among the British middle managers.

Twenty-three of the thirty German middle managers had completed technical or commercial apprenticeships after taking the equivalent of O-levels (see Table 3.1). Of these, seven had later acquired further formal qualifications by completing a degree programme at a polytechnic or professional academy. The remaining seven had stayed on to complete their *Abitur* and had gone on to university. Only one manager completed an apprenticeship as well as a university degree (see Table 3.2).

The relevance of apprenticeships to German management is endorsed by the high incidence of one-time apprentices at the highest levels of industry. 55 per cent of the senior executives studied by Eberwein and Tholen had completed a commercial or technical apprenticeship.[8]

Among the British managers studied, the distinctive element was the predominance of professional qualifications, sometimes on top of

Table 3.1   Vocational training of German middle managers
              (apprenticeship)

Vocational training level	Total	Percentage of total
No vocational training (apprenticeship)	6	20.0
Commercial training	20	66.7
Technical training	4	13.3
Total	30	100.0

Table 3.2   Academic degrees received by German middle managers

Academic degree	Total	Percentage of total
None	17	56.6
Professional academy (*Berufsakademie*)	2	6.7
Polytechnic (*Fachhochschule*)	5	16.7
University	6	20.0
Total	30	100.0

university degrees. Five of the six degree-holders were also members of their professional institutions. The completion of a relevant degree would have exempted them from certain modules in their professional qualification.

Altogether, sixteen of the thirty middle managers were members of professional institutes. In national terms, this figure is disproportionately high, reflecting the strong professional tradition in our three industries (brewing, insurance and construction). Nevertheless, it reflects the larger developmental role played by professional institutes in Britain (see Table 3.3).

It is also interesting to note that in terms of academic degrees the qualification profile of the British middle managers in our sample compares favourably with that of their German counterparts. This is

Table 3.3   Highest qualification attained by the British middle managers

Qualification	Middle managers	Percentage of total
First higher degree	6	20.0
Member of professional institution	11	36.6
HNC/HND	0	0
Apprenticeship	2	6.7
ONC/OND, City & Guilds, A-levels	5	16.7
O-levels or equivalent	3	10.0
CSE	1	3.3
None	2	6.7
Total	30	100.0

surprising in view of the preceding commentary about the academic bias of German management.

The qualification profile of the two sets of bosses interviewed favours the Germans. Of the eight British senior managers, four had a degree, three were members of professional institutions, and one had only O-levels. Among the thirteen German senior managers, two had doctorates and nine were either university or polytechnic graduates. The other two had both completed commercial apprenticeships.

These comparisons suggest a wider gap between the qualification profile of middle and top managers in Germany, than occurs in Britain. This finding is corroborated by several studies of German senior managers. Hartmann,[9] Zapf,[10] Kruk,[11] Evers,[12] Poensgen,[13] and Wuppermann,[14] have all shown that senior managers have significantly higher formal qualifications than those of the middle managers in our survey. A more recent study, by Eberwein and Tholen,[15] found that, among the top two layers of corporate executives – that is, including the first level of managers below the board – only 18 per cent had received no tertiary education. Of the rest, 16 per cent had graduated from a professional academy or polytechnic, and 66 per cent from a university, with an impressive 24 per cent also holding a doctorate.

In our study, there was evidence that qualifications played a significant role in propelling people through the organization, but the effect was more marked in Germany. Among the German managers, there were considerable differences in career speed. Those middle managers with only a technical or commercial apprenticeship to their name, stayed in each job for an average of eight years. Those who had acquired further training at a technical or professional academy fared little better, remaining in their previous positions for approximately seven years. Those middle managers with university degrees, on the other hand, moved on far quicker. They stayed in their former positions for an average of four years.

Among the British managers, a slightly different picture emerged. Of the six graduates, only two were clearly identifiable as fast-trackers. These two (one in insurance and one in construction) had both changed positions at an accelerated rate. The insurance manager was 29 years old and had held nine positions in eight years, her longest one being twenty months. The construction manager was 32-years-old and had held eight positions in eleven years, the longest one being three years.

Of the four remaining graduates, two in technical roles had apparently remained on a plateau, and two were in '*cul-de-sac*' functions – one was a quality manager, the other a training manager – without obvious career ladders. None of these four had experienced a job change in the previous three years, which in the British context is a long time.

Qualifications clearly play some part in a manager's advancement in Britain, but they offer no guarantee. An absence of qualifications need not bar access to the higher reaches of management in Britain. A survey by Peter Herriot of 753 junior, middle and senior managers in Britain showed that 'non-graduates are promoted higher than graduates'.[16] A striking example, in our own study, was the insurance-company director with only five O-levels (and only five years experience of the insurance industry). In Britain, then, a manager's formal qualification is a far weaker determinant of likely career-advancement opportunities, than in Germany. However, the importance attached to formal qualifications will vary with the industry and the company.

The different weighting accorded to qualifications in the two countries had an interesting impact on managerial outlook. There seemed to be a greater sense of predestination in German careers. German middle managers were more likely to hit a glass ceiling because of paucity of formal qualifications. By comparison, British managers will not find themselves excluded from top management simply on the strength of educational credentials, but there is a downside attached to this greater openness.

Management performance is not easily measurable. Promotion criteria can therefore seem arbitrary and unfair. One sensed greater resentment at being passed over among the British middle managers than among their German colleagues. This resentment manifested itself in their explanations of career success. When asked what is the key to success, British managers readily invoked 'being in the right place at the right time', 'your face fitting', 'it's not what you know, but who you know' and so on. One explanation may be that in Britain managers expect to move jobs every few years whereas the German middle managers stay longer in the same post. There is also a stronger educational barrier to top management in Germany than in Britain. For both these reasons some British middle managers may be more likely to have a sense of grievance at not being promoted. Yet another reason may be that leadership and managerial ability are seen as more important for promotion in Britain and such qualities are harder to identify clearly than technical abilities. As Mant observed, the British system can lead to a virtuous circle whereby 'advancement is taken as *evidence* of suitability for further advancement up the ladder'.[17] In the German model, promotion is based to a large extent on tangible and quantifiable criteria as embodied in qualifications. As a sifting device, these may be questionable, but at least they are known and understood by all.

In Britain, qualifications also play less of a role in determining the functional responsibilities of managers. One of the insurance managers in our sample was a chemistry graduate, while one of the personnel managers had graduated as a production engineer. An article in *The Independent* confirmed this widespread practice:

> Britain – unlike other European countries – has a long-established tradition of recruiting graduates of any discipline. About half of all opportunities are open to graduates of 'any discipline'.[18]

Later in the same article, the national recruitment partner for Touche Ross, the accountancy firm, observed:

> Only about 20 per cent of our graduate intake has a relevant qualification in accountancy these days; a quarter has an arts degree.[19]

In the German companies studied there was a much stronger relationship in the sample between the formal qualifications of the managers and their functional responsibilities. For instance, all the middle managers in the German insurance company had completed an apprenticeship as insurance agents. As Randlesome observes:

> German companies perceive the management task in strictly functional terms, especially for middle and lower managers. Hence the direct relationship between vocational training or studies and the job to be done is of the utmost significance.[20]

In the British context, educational requirements were not only looser, they were sometimes disregarded. There was a weak relationship between actual and ideal qualifications as stipulated in the job description.

Job Descriptions and Qualifications

We can make few comparisons between German and British job descriptions since only one of the three German companies, the insurance company, had them. In this company the job descriptions covered the main features of the job, qualification requirements and a description of the main tasks to be performed by the incumbent. There was a strong emphasis on the qualifications required for the job, so that potential applicants had to be developed towards acquiring these before they were promoted.

The British job descriptions gave educational prerequisites. However, in each of the three British companies there was a striking willingness to ignore prescribed qualifications if the 'right candidate' did not happen to possess them. While the resulting comparison is unflattering we can learn more from focusing on the people who fall short in each company, than by looking at those who meet the educational standards.

In the brewery, job incumbents generally fell short of the specified educational threshold (in seven out of ten cases). In a number of instances, the phrasing specified a particular qualification but indicated a willingness to settle for less. For instance, 'Desirable to be educated to degree standard' or 'Preferably member of Chartered Institute of Transport'.

The most notable transgression was the brewing and fermenting manager who was the first such manager in the works who was neither a graduate nor qualified by the Institute of Brewing. While this made him exceptional, the fact that he was doing this job and that he was accepted in that role, is noteworthy, even if it is unusual. In Germany he could not have been appointed even as a 'caretaker' manager as this man was (though the appointment was later confirmed).

In the insurance company, qualifications were generally not mentioned, since most employees join the company straight from school and are trained within it. But, in the few instances where specific requirements are mentioned (actuarial, finance), they may, in practice, be ignored. A striking example is that of the wholly unqualified Financial Accountant whose job description explicitly states: 'An appropriate professional accounting qualification is essential.' This is doubly surprising considering the high number of qualified accountants in Britain.

In the construction company, qualifications were not mentioned but the background of some of the managers is worth highlighting. The Purchasing Manager was not a member of a professional institute and had no A-levels; the Regional Estimating Manager had no professional qualification (was not a qualified Quantity Surveyor); and one Technical Manager had no post-school qualifications other than an apprenticeship in carpentry.

These examples show a more relaxed attitude to the importance of qualifications as an indication of job competence than that which prevails in Germany. It also shows that British companies are not constrained by the contents of job descriptions, which serve as guidelines rather than rule books.

Management Training and Development

The executive training programmes initiated by the German firms in our study were geared towards enhancing the technical understanding of the managers. Twenty-three of the thirty middle managers stated that they participated in seminars and training programmes which improved technical skills directly related to their position, while only ten of the managers had taken part in what they could label management seminars.

Executive training programmes for the British managers, seemed more evenly balanced between the acquisition of managerial and technical skills. In addition to skills in employment law (training manager), developing purchasing skills (purchasing manager), total quality management (TQM) (renewals manager), warehouse management and materials handling (distribution manager), there were general training courses (often externally run) on: man-management skills, communications, presentation skills, managing teams, leadership, project management, finance and strategy, managing change and assertiveness.

German companies place more emphasis on the applicable contents of training courses. They are less likely to view the training period as a useful period of reflection, or to use training as a motivator (perhaps when promotion or remuneration are unavailable). Training in German companies is firmly need-driven rather than status or reward-driven.[21]

Career Moves

Table 3.4 shows the number of years each set of managers had spent with their current employer.

The fortuitous similarity between British and German figures in Table 3.4, gives an added edge to the comparisons which follow.

Approximately two-thirds of the German middle managers in our study had spent their entire professional careers working in only one

Table 3.4 Length of time with current employer

Length of time	British managers	German managers
up to 10 years	5	4
11 to 20 years	8	8
more than 20 years	17	18
Total	30	30

firm. Of those who had moved around, only four (out of thirty) had moved more than once − and even then, it was always between companies in the same sector.

The British middle managers, like their German counterparts, tended to have been with their companies for many years, generally more than ten. None of them had been with their company for less than six years. Nine of the thirty had experience of other industries, but this tended to be early on in their careers. Nine had experience of other companies in the same industry, but again this tended to be early on in their careers. None of the managers had been with more than four companies. Twelve of the thirty managers had spent their entire careers with the same company.

The career background of the British middle-management group was different from that of the German group − notably in the fact that one third had experienced work in another sector − but the differences are not as striking as might be expected. What *The Times* described as 'The British manager's traditional love affair with mobility'[22] is not borne out by our study. Admittedly, this has a lot to do with the prevailing ethos within the sectors studied (brewing, insurance and construction); but it may suggest that those who reach senior management move between companies or sectors more than do middle managers.

The notion that career differences between British and German managers are perhaps more pronounced at senior-management level can be illustrated by the Management Development Manager of the British insurance company. She explained:

Five or six years ago, we recruited a lot of people from outside the industry to fill vacancies at senior level. This was because we had not paid enough attention to developing people within the company.

As a consequence, the most long-serving of the company's three executive directors had been with the company for just four years; and only one of these three had been recruited from within the insurance sector. The Management Development Manager was aiming to fill one-third of senior executive vacancies from outside the company and two-thirds with insiders.

While the circumstances were no doubt exceptional, one can ill-imagine any of the German companies so cheerfully welcoming executives who were not only new to the company, but also to the industry. This is certainly a practice which is more established in Britain. It reflects the lucidity and sense of detachment which outsiders are deemed to bring to organizations, the widespread belief in the transferability of management practice, and the favourable view of mobility as an indication of drive and a source of experience.

In contrast with this, the German senior managers in our study did not have significantly different career patterns from their middle-management colleagues, as far as mobility between companies is concerned, and this is confirmed by other studies. 76 per cent of the executives surveyed by Zapf,[23] and 53 per cent of those studied by Eberwein and Tholen,[24] had either not changed firms or had changed only once in the course of their career. The same sort of pattern emerged among the more senior German managers in our study.

While the British middle managers in our study did not show much greater propensity to change employers than did their German counterparts, they did move around more within their companies (see Table 3.5).

Table 3.5 shows a marked difference between the British and German middle managers in the time spent in present job. Two-

Table 3.5 Length of time the middle managers had held their current position

	British managers	German managers
Less than 2 years	13	3
2 to 4 years	12	7
5 to 9 years	4	8
10 to 19 years	1	6
20 or more years	0	6
	30	30

thirds of the German middle managers in our study had held their current position for more than five years, as opposed to only one-sixth of the British managers – a significant difference,[25] given the preceding similarity in the time each set of managers had spent with their current employer (see Table 3.4).

The extent to which our findings are typical is corroborated by Wheatley's study of British Institute of Management (BIM) members.[26] His sample of over 1000 middle managers showed that 36 per cent of managers had been in their present position for less than 2 years; that 26 per cent had been there for 2–4 years; 14 per cent for 4–6 years; and the remainder for over 6 years.

The British skew towards spending less time in the job is interesting on two counts. First, it reflects the greater scope for movement in the more heavily layered British companies. Second, it reflects Anglo-Saxon thinking about managerial motivation, and the importance of a fresh challenge, over the steady accumulation of experience. As the Director of Human Resources in the British construction company observed:

> The perceived view here is that you do not try to leave somebody, even at fairly senior level, longer than seven years with the same set of wallpaper – if only to keep them stimulated.

The widely accepted view in Britain is that once a job is mastered, the manager needs a change of scenery to avoid stagnation – and to avoid blocking the career development of promising managers. The question 'What have been the main changes in your job in the last year?' often prompted the response, 'I have only been in the job for eight months'. Movement was rapid and unannounced. Often there had been significant changes in status between the interview and the observation phases. In Germany, they seem to place a premium on the expertise and trust that builds up over a long time and less on variety of experience or on the idea of motivation through mobility.

The greater internal mobility of British managers is also made possible by the previously mentioned fact that jobs are less tied to qualifications. If the two are strongly linked, then the scope for lateral movement is inevitably limited. This would appear to be the case in Germany, where all the middle managers bar one had experience of only one functional area, within their current firm. The one middle manager who has not remained in the same department under his present employer moved from the Marketing department to the Sales division – hardly a radical departure in view of the old chestnut about marketing being 'sales with a college education'.

The notion of a *Kaminkarriere* where middle managers remain in the same functional area of a firm throughout their working life is a familiar one in Germany. Indeed, the fact that the Germans have a name for it suggests that. The findings of other authors show that this phenomenon is typical in other sectors, besides the ones studied. 'Horizontal mobility', according to Dröll and Dröll,[27] as well as Pippke and Wolfmeyer,[28] was virtually unknown within the firms which they studied.

In contrast with this, Nicholson and West found that 10 per cent of job changes in their British study of 2300 managers were internal lateral moves.[29] Perhaps, even more surprising was the fact that around 75 per cent of all job changes (whether internal or external, upwards or downwards) involved a change of function.

In Britain, mobility is clearly regarded as an integral part of career development:

> Large companies have traditionally prepared cohorts of potential senior managers by moving people every 18 months or so between jobs and functions.[30]

Even now that opportunities are reduced with fewer layers, British companies still believe in 'broadening' managers through project work and by involvement in more strategic forums such as steering committees.

In Germany, there was far less emphasis on mobility and development through exposure to different situations. The fact that German middle managers spent very much longer in their jobs suggests that expertise is more highly valued than variety of experience, at least at the middle-management level.

All this reveals an interesting difference in the British and German views of what management is about. It indicates the relative importance of general (people) as opposed to specific (tasks) experience as a quality of middle management. In Germany you do not manage, you manage something.

It also highlights an area of management, namely comparative mobility, its benefits and implications, which tends to be under-researched.

SUMMARY

Overall, then, it could be said that the different views of the importance of formal qualifications, with all their consequences for career mobility and the view of management, may be regarded as one of the key differences between British and German middle managers.

4 Demands, Constraints and Choices of Middle Managers' Jobs

This chapter sets out to explore how the British and German managers see their jobs. This will be done using Stewart's model, described fully in Chapter 1. The spotlight will be placed, in turn, on the demands, the constraints and the choices perceived by our two sets of managers.

WHAT A MANAGER HAS TO DO (DEMANDS)

There are many aspects of a manager's job over which he or she has no choice. As a rule, meeting these *demands* is no guarantee of success in the job, but not meeting them may well constitute failure. Some of these obligations are set out as responsibilities or compulsory contacts in the job description; others are agreed with the boss as objectives; and others still are communicated informally by the boss, peers or subordinates as expectations.

There is a consensus among the British and German middle managers in the study as to the nature of the core requirement: it is *to run their area smoothly*.

> Effectiveness to my boss is whether I keep him out of trouble and make his life easier. (Contracts Manager, British construction company)

> My boss's first priority is that his department runs smoothly, and the second is, of course, that my office runs smoothly and that I bother him as little as possible with petty matters. (Claims Processing Manager, German insurance company)

> The business has to run smoothly, positively. And when there are visible improvements in all that one does . . . That's when I feel I'm working most effectively for the firm. (Sales Manager, German brewery)

For things to run smoothly, there are two main requirements on which the two sets of managers also agree: the employees have to be motivated and there has to be a good working climate within the department. Ensuring that both of these conditions are satisfied is also the responsibility of the manager.

> Maintaining a good spirit in the tender team. If people are unhappy or feel they are being treated poorly then they are not going to work efficiently. (Estimating Manager, British construction company)

> Just being together, because that is, after all, the requirement for being able to achieve everything that we have as our goals. (Sales Manager, German brewery)

> To motivate everyone, and everything that goes along with that, to ensure that you are in a favourable position. (Customer Services Manager, German insurance company)

The Balance of Managerial, Technical and Administrative Responsibilities

Behind this superficial similarity, however, there lie important differences of emphasis – particularly, in the perceived balance of managerial and technical responsibilities. The British managers place far more stress than their German counterparts on the ability to motivate their subordinates. The phrase 'man-management' was often used to encapsulate the difficulties of the job, to describe the fundamental requirement of any managerial position, and to explain the relative effectiveness of different managers. Among the German managers, the motivation of the team was seen far less as the personal and sole responsibility of the manager. It was also seen more as a means to an end – namely the fulfilling of technical responsibilities – rather than as an end in itself.

A more striking difference still can be seen in the administrative responsibilities of the two sets of managers. This is particularly noticeable in their budgetary workload. British managers are typically assigned a budget which covers their complete departmental costs, such as wages and salaries, overtime pay, refurbishment allowance, spending on equipment and office consumables and so on. In German companies single departmental budgets are more the exception than the rule. For British managers, then, the preparation and submission of budgets for approval, followed by the adminis-tration of the allocated funds, is an additional demand that must be met, beyond the general technical and managerial responsibilities.

This demand on the British managers would seem to result in more choice, relative to their German counterparts, in decision-making, but this impression is largely illusory. The British managers were not free to spend their budget as they pleased. The funds were fairly strictly allocated and only minor sums may be shifted across headings, with a deliberate saving in one area off-setting an overspend in another.

Even the recruitment of new employees, which some British middle managers consider to be necessary to organize their departments differently, is rarely an option within the existing budget. Not surprisingly, then, the budget agreement is viewed by many of the British managers, as an unduly laborious process not justified by the size of the discretionary element in the budget. Once the key elements such as staffing costs and systems charges have been deducted, the remainder is fairly small. It is also felt that the budgets are too compartmentalized so that, even out of the discretionary residue, it is not easy to spend money on what heads of department feel is necessary.

Yet, one must not overlook the psychological importance, in Britain at least, of being in charge of a budget. It is a recognized symbol of managerial status. Such signals are particularly important in British organizations where managers are not systematically distinguished from their subordinates by either expertise or qualifica-tions. For many British managers, it is the size of the budget, not the nature of the responsibilities, that reflects the scale of the job.

The Explicitness of Role Expectations

A further difference between middle managers in Britain and Germany can be seen in the formalization of role expectations. All three British companies in the study were able to provide job descriptions for the managerial jobs studied. Some of these made extremely detailed demands of the jobholder. For instance, the job description for the purchasing manager in the British construction company actually stipulated that the incumbent should have a sense of humour! (see Appendix 2). Of the German companies, only the insurance company currently had job descriptions.

Taken at face value, this would suggest that the demands made of the jobholder are more standardized in Britain than in Germany. If we look at what actually happens though, it transpires that few of these so-called demands are very binding in Britain, and occasionally may be ignored completely.

A less rigid view of formal job requirements in Britain is accompanied by a more malleable view of organizational structures. The British managers in our study showed a readiness to make minor modifications to the organizational structure in order to accommodate people's abilities and experience, and to overcome their shortcomings: the job is adapted to the person rather than vice versa. For instance, the distribution manager in the British brewery was also supposed to be computer-literate in order to handle the logistics of the operation. His inability to use a computer did not stop him getting the job. The job was simply split into two with the logistics part being hived off to a colleague. The rationale behind this was that it was less important to have someone who could adequately discharge both aspects of the job, than someone who could deal with the trade unions – and, as a former shop steward, he was well-qualified. The willingness to shape jobs to the managers' individual characteristics can partly be explained by the low level of standardization in the British education system (see Chapter 4).

The pattern in Germany is very different. The high standardization of training for jobs through the qualification system means that it is often unnecessary to spell out what is required of the jobholder. If you are the head of production in a brewing company, then you will have undergone a technical apprenticeship in a brewery, and you will be a graduate in brewing studies and have a number of years of experience in that particular function. There is no need to state explicitly the necessary qualifications, experience and abilities of the jobholder since these are taken for granted – no one who falls short of these requirements would even dream of applying for the job. In Britain, they need to be stated because they are merely guidelines – an ideal profile which will often be modified and can be ignored.

The apparent formalization of job specifications in Britain, then, can be misleading. About the only managerial requirement on which British companies insist – and in many ways it is the least verifiable – is the ability to handle people. Thus, the demands made of middle managers in Britain do not have a lot to do with meeting the technical requirements laid out in job descriptions. Rather it is a question of meeting the expectations of role-senders, notably those of the immediate boss.

The jobholder is not just a passive recipient of expectations. In Britain more than in Germany expectations are negotiable. People's perceptions of what is effective (and ineffective) behaviour can be reshaped. So the particular nature of those expectations is largely dependent on the negotiation skills of the jobholder. Indeed, it is essential for newly appointed managers to review the norms set by their predecessors, and to gear the expectations of the boss (as well as peers and subordinates) towards their own particular strengths.

That is more necessary in Britain where job rotation is far higher than in Germany, and where managerial jobs are more readily redesigned. This constant flux and uncertainty makes it important for British managers to communicate and redefine their job responsibilities in regular one-to-one meetings with their bosses. The speed with which jobs and incumbents change in Britain, means that job descriptions are constantly trying to catch up with job activities rather than driving or shaping them. For instance, the Finance Manager in the British insurance company had effectively become the Special Projects Manager although he retained overall responsibility for financial production. But those financial tasks were actually handled by a specially appointed subordinate.

In the British brewery, the key tasks of the job were refocused annually in agreement with the boss. Meetings of this sort, where the key tasks of the jobholder are redefined, were much rarer in the German companies in our study. The annual goals for the German managers were more likely to relate to financial measures of costs and profit-making responsibility.

It is further worth noting that both sets of managers were required to take on additional tasks which fell outside their normal responsibilities. Where possible these would be included in the annual objectives of the British managers – but if, for reasons of timing, they could not be integrated into written objectives, it did not pose a problem. The annual objectives could be renegotiated informally. It is conceivable that this mismatch between written expectations and actual responsibilities would have been intolerable in the German companies.

The less-institutionalized communication of expectations and objectives in Germany does not necessarily mean that German middle managers are less aware of what is expected of them. The formal and explicit communication of expectations is not essential as it is in Britain. As was noted in Chapter 3, German managers generally spend longer in their jobs, they experience a slow rate of promotion within one functional area, and they do not really go in for inter-company mobility. This guarantees continuity and stability in the management structure, which makes frequent and comprehensive communication of role expectations superfluous. The bosses of the German middle managers explicitly stated that the communication of expectations is restricted to two situations: first, when a subordinate takes over a new job and second, when the incumbent does not fulfil the boss's expectations.

Who the Managers Must Talk To

Demands arise for both British and German managers from the cooperation requirements associated with their positions. But there are wide differences between all the managers in the nature and frequency of their compulsory contacts with other people. Some of these stem from differences in function; others, from differences in organizational structure and others still from differences in market conditions.

The differences in compulsory contacts between managers in different functions are, of course, to be expected. From the patterns of telephone contact in our study, it is apparent that managers in the administration and finance functions are obliged to have the most contact with head office (reporting results upwards); those in production have the widest number of contacts within the unit or subsidiary (high cooperation requirements); and those in sales will have the most contact with people outside the company (especially customers).

This study is less concerned with the differences *within* companies than those *between* companies and, of course, *between countries*. So we focused on the differences between the production departments of the twinned companies in each sector. We chose production because of its centrality to the operation and because of its high dependency on other departments. This tells us a lot about the demands imposed by the organizational structure (see Chapter 2 for organizational charts of the companies) and the market place. What follows are paired comparisons of the British and German companies in each sector.

Brewing industry
In both countries the breweries were organized by function: maintenance, production, packaging, distribution and so on. There is a critical difference in structure, however, which increases the cooperation requirements for three of the British managers. In Britain, the packaging and production managers report to the same boss, but the

maintenance manager reports to a different boss. The three functions only come together at managing director level. In Germany, the packaging, production and maintenance managers all report to the same boss. Inevitably, he judges them not just on their individual performances, but also on how well they work together. This means that there is an in-built incentive for them to cooperate with one another – and individual clashes of interest can easily be reconciled according to the needs of the unit.

This strict segregation of the production and maintenance functions was typical of British firms.[1] In the British brewery it had repercussions on the number and nature of daily meetings. In Germany, the heads of production, packaging and maintenance would all get together for 20–30 minutes each day to coordinate their activities. For instance, they would discuss at what time of the day specific pieces of equipment should be serviced, as well as discussing technical breakdowns and short-term changes in production plans.

In the British brewery, there were two daily maintenance meetings, one with production and one with packaging. In Germany these meetings were combined into a single meeting. In both countries these meetings tended to last less than 30 minutes, but there was an important difference in style. A much greater element of persuasion was needed in the British meetings because they involved a higher level of routine negotiation. In the British brewery the segregation of maintenance from the other two departments meant that they had different priorities and objectives. This segregation can be traced back to the boundaries between the different trade unions at shop-floor level.

While the system of industrial relations in Germany is made up of industry-based trade unions, the British industrial relations system is characterized by multi-unionism. Inevitably this gives rise to job demarcation problems and occasional conflict, and it introduces a certain rigidity in how work can be organized.[2] It also poses problems for the British middle managers in their departments. They feel pressure from below to represent their subordinates' interests while, at the same time, feeling pressure from above to cooperate fully with other departments.

In contrast with the German brewery, then, managers in the British brewery found personnel issues were a constant feature of their daily meetings. The packaging manager, for instance, raised one demarcation problem with his maintenance counterpart, where packaging operatives were unwilling to let maintenance workers fill the water-tanks. The problem for the packaging operatives was not that this task required special skills, but that letting someone else do it eroded their jobs – something which was of particular concern in an environment of recession.

The maintenance manager retaliated with a grievance of his own. He reported on discontent among his 'lads' about doing maintenance, as opposed to breakdowns. He explained that the shop stewards had complained to him that it did not feature in the job descriptions! What is a matter of routine in Germany, becomes a management issue in Britain.

The more pronounced separation between production and maintenance clearly makes higher demands of cooperation between the managers in the British brewery than in the German one. But the reverse is true of the relationship between sales and production. This can be traced back to differences between the sales markets in Britain and Germany. While beer in Britain is mostly sold in barrels and served on tap in pubs and restaurants, most beer in Germany is bottled or canned and sold in retail or wholesale outlets.[3]

The German brewery therefore has to be much more responsive to a dynamic/competitive market-place, since, compared to the British brewery, it has only a few 'tied' outlets which guarantee steady levels of sales. Within the German brewery this causes an inevitable clash of interests between the production departments (brewing and packaging) and the distribution and sales functions.

> The sales department wants everything at once, but that is impossible, we cannot fill all types of bottle at once. (Packaging Manager, German brewery)

For instance, meetings between the packaging manager and the sales department occur less frequently but are more difficult. In these meetings, which last about one hour, there are many conflicts of interest.

The German distribution department must constantly react to new or changed orders from the sales department. This often means that the packaging department has to modify production schedules at short notice. Different beers, different bottles, different production runs have to be juggled by the packaging manager to meet the needs of distribution and to fulfil the orders obtained by sales.

Inevitably this causes tension. Switches in packaging take time in terms of refitting the bottling facilities, and these demands conflict with the packaging manager's own volume-objectives. The demands downstream also mean that the packaging manager has to coordinate properly upstream, with the production department, to make sure that the right sort of beer is available to be bottled. In this respect, the packaging and production departments are very much at the beck and call of the sales function. It is a feature of the way the industry is structured.

In Britain, the market is not competitive in the same way. Relatively speaking, the British brewery was production-, rather than sales-driven. The packaging manager in Britain benefited not just from a less-dynamic market, but also from a standardized form of packaging, namely barrels (which do not require labelling either). The coordination requirements, in this respect, were far higher in the German brewery than in the British one – though the German brewery was powerless to change this industry-wide characteristic.

Insurance industry
The differences between the cooperation requirements in the German and British insurance firms are even more striking than those in the breweries.

In the insurance industry, the equivalent of production was the customer services division, where policies were processed or modified and sent out. In the British company, this unit was split into separate functions including new business, existing business, renewals (premium-chasing), alterations and surrenders. It was the heads of these departments that we observed.

In the German company, these customer service operations were broken up, not by function, but according to policy end-numbers. This meant that a given customer would always deal with the same unit (and even clerk) whatever the operation required, whether altering a policy or making a claim. In the German insurance company, all the operations were integrated.

This integration of operations can be traced back to two factors. First, the highly regulated German insurance market allows the work of the insurance clerks to be highly standardized as well as making it more amenable to the full exploitation of new information and communication technologies. Second, the thorough apprenticeship served by German clerks means that they are able to handle a wider range of operations than their British counterparts.

The impact of this difference in structure, on the cooperation requirements, was significant. A simple comparison of the number of periodic meetings the managers were required to attend is telling. Relative to their 'production' counterparts in the German brewing and construction companies, the German customer service managers were involved in far fewer and shorter meetings. For instance, there was only one meeting a month where all the office managers met with their bosses, and that lasted between one and two hours.

The nature of those meetings was also quite different from those in the German brewing and construction companies which revolved around the coordination of the work of the various units. Customer service meetings concentrated more on achieving consistency between the units in the way that unusual cases were handled.

> The reason for the meetings is that the offices have to be coordinated. All offices are doing the same things (have the same tasks) – or as I should say – should do the same things. But there is a certain scope of choice for each office manager, and therefore we have to formulate general routines, so that we do it in the same way. (Office Manager, Customer Services, German insurance company)

Besides that formal contact in meetings, there was little contact between the colleagues in parallel departments. What little additional contact was necessary was primarily to exchange information and to take advantage of the expert knowledge of colleagues.

The cooperation requirements in the British insurance firm were far heavier than those in the German insurance firm. With each department having quite separate technical responsibilities, the need for coordination at middle-management level was greater than in the German insurance company. Naturally, this led to longer and more frequent meetings. There was a regular weekly meeting between the heads of functions and their boss which lasted between two and three hours. On top of that, there were numerous *ad hoc* meetings between the colleagues in pairs.

There were also numerous meetings with the managers from the quality assurance and technical support functions. These functions could be regarded as the insurance company's equivalent of maintenance in production companies. Again, this segregation of functions which, in Germany, are integrated, was a recurrent theme in the British companies studied.

Construction industry
Of the three sectors, the two companies in the construction industry showed the greatest similarity in their cooperation requirements. This can be explained by the fact that the organizational structures of these two companies were the most similar.

Despite the differences described in Chapter 2 each division (or subdivision) was in charge of all the construction sites within it. The managers we observed were the technical managers (called contract managers in Britain) and the commercial managers (called managing quantity surveyors in Britain).

Contact among the technical managers, and contact among the commercial managers was fairly insignificant. The critical relationship was that between the technical manager (contracts manager) and the commercial manager (managing quantity surveyor) in charge of each project. They met regularly in formal production meetings as well as being in constant informal contact to discuss technical, financial or people problems which may arise.

In both countries, meetings were very much project-driven. The joint contribution of the technical and commercial managers was especially important during the tender process and in setting up and closing projects.

The cooperation requirements, then, for the middle managers in both countries were broadly similar. But there was one important difference in the cooperation between the technical and commercial managers. In the German firm, the technical and commercial managers were constant partners. They were jointly responsible for all construction projects allotted to them. This meant that constant communication and cooperation were built into the structure. In the British company, one technical manager would have different commercial partners depending on the size of the project and the workloads of those managers. Likewise, each commercial manager would be paired up with different technical managers. One of the technical managers observed had worked with up to five different commercial counterparts on the various projects for which he was responsible. Because of this complexity in structure, there was not the same continuity of relationships as in Germany. It also meant that there were more likely to be clashes of priorities over which projects were seen to require the most attention.

The technical and commercial managers in both countries were also in more frequent contact with outside constituencies than their counterparts in the other industries. External contacts such as subcontractors, clients, architects, and design teams made significant demands on the time of the middle managers in construction. These relationships were deemed critical to the financial success of a project. It was important for the middle managers to build up a rapport when things were running smoothly in case there were problems later.

The technical managers also had an increasing requirement to get involved in the acquisition of new business. This entailed greater involvement in marketing events/functions as well as a higher profile at the tender stage – the technical manager forming a vital part of the package on offer to the client. Again, the construction industry is unusual in this respect. In other industries 'production' managers are very rarely in direct contact with end-users.

That contact with the client was partly cosmetic, in that the technical manager is not on site, yet it continued throughout the contract. Clients increasingly expect to have access to the technical and commercial managers with overall responsibility for the project – and expect them to intervene personally if there are problems on site.

Structural differences affecting cooperation   An interesting theme, in the cooperation requirements, transcends all three industries. It is the recurrent pattern of German integration versus British specialization.

The three German companies all seemed intent on building cooperation into the structure: first, by having a common boss who judged the performance of the potentially conflicting managers on the way that they worked together; second, by organizing independent units which worked in parallel, rather than in sequence; and third, by making sure that the same technical and commercial managers were always paired on the same projects.

In contrast with this, the British companies tended to break down tasks into separate functions. Inevitably, this requires an additional coordination effort and generates more liaison meetings in Britain. A striking example of this organizational fragmentation was the existence, in all three British companies, of independent quality functions. In the German companies, quality was not split off from the central production processes: it was built-in not bolted-on.

Nor was cooperation helped in Britain by the way that objectives were set up. The fact that they focused on the individual was good for 'ownership' and accountability, but it did not help cooperation in the way that collective objectives might have done. On several occasions during the study, British managers were asked to do things which, though in the interests of the unit, would impede their own objectives. Getting them to agree to such a course of action inevitably involved more negotiation and persuasion.

Having considered the various demands made of the managers studied, we can now consider some of the ways in which they felt constrained.

CONSTRAINTS

Environmental Constraints

While the idea of demands, constraints and choices provides a useful way of comparing jobs, the three categories are not always clear-cut. For instance, what some managers perceive as demands may actually be things they have chosen to do, especially where non-delegation is concerned. Drawing the line between demands and constraints can also prove difficult since they are often two sides of the same coin, as we shall see.

The dominant constraint cited by both sets of managers was the economic environment. This is odd in view of the contrasting economic situations of the two countries at the time of the study, with Britain deep in recession and Germany boosted by the opening-up of the former East German market.

In both countries the prevailing economic environment not only constrained the managers' ability to structure their work – it also made certain demands on the managers. For the British middle managers, working in a recessionary context imposed limitations on the financial initiatives they could take, as well as forcing them to concentrate on cost-effectiveness. For instance, in the British brewery the middle managers were expected to reduce staffing costs by limiting overtime and not replacing retiring staff. In the British construction company, the middle managers were required to pass on the reduced margins on contracts to subcontractors and suppliers, and to drive projects hard in order to keep them profitable. In the British insurance company, there was tightening of expense allowances and increased scrutiny of costs, especially staffing costs.

These financial constraints also had repercussions on how the managers handled their staff. The threat of redundancy, the low pay increases and the reduced business volumes meant that staff morale in the British companies was low. This made particular demands on the interpersonal sensitivity of the British middle managers. For instance, the construction managers went round to the sites personally to hand out the small or non-existent personal bonuses (normally bonus awards were simply sent out through the internal post).

The need for heightened sensitivity also manifested itself in the British insurance company, when it came to clamping down on the practice of paying premiums by cheque, rather than through direct debit. Policy holders were normally granted a grace period of three months during which they could pay by cheque. But this period had been stretched by lenient clerks who sympathized with the personal predicaments of some of the policy-holders. This was costing the company more money in processing costs and there was also the risk of the practice becoming widespread, so it had to be brought to a halt. Rather than do this in a high-handed way, by simply enforcing the regulations, the renewals manager gathered all the section leaders for an open discussion. This enabled them to air their views and for the renewals manager to explain why the practice had to stop.

The situation in the German companies differed considerably. Here, economic growth had led to increased business volumes and much higher workloads for the German middle managers and their staff. If anything, these excessive workloads were even more of a constraint on the creative possibilities of the German managers than budgetary limitations were on their British counterparts.

Almost every German middle manager complained about lack of personnel or of excessive workloads. As in Britain, this also had implications for the way that the German managers handled their subordinates. It was incumbent on the managers to motivate their staff to sustain their efforts in the face of so much work, and also to persuade them to work overtime and on weekends.

A more surprising, but not unrelated constraint mentioned by the German managers in all three industries was that their staff were underqualified. For the German managers to complain about the inadequacies of their staff seems odd given the much-praised apprenticeship system and the high proportion of employees with job-related qualifications. The complaint is all the more surprising given that none of the British managers cited the technical shortcomings of their staff as a constraining factor.

This difference in perspective has two possible explanations. First, the high-standardization of professional training in Germany may mean that middle managers have developed inordinate expectations of what subordinates should be able to do. The argument is reversible for Britain, where managers have relatively low technical expectations of their subordinates because of the low level of standardization of professional training. Indeed, that pattern is repeated at managerial level, as evidenced by the accepted failure of the British managers to meet the full technical specifications for their jobs. This shortfall did not, as far as we could tell, preoccupy the bosses of those middle managers either. A second explanation for German sensitivity to staff inadequacies relates back to the lack of personnel. Given similar levels of 'output' of beer produced, policies handled, and construction volume, the British companies in our study had significantly more personnel than the German companies. With less 'slack' in personnel, it is understandable that the German managers should feel more exposed to skill shortages.

At the same time, the German middle managers observed found themselves trapped in a vicious circle. Because of the demands on them, they did not have the time to train their employees properly. The demands of the workload therefore generated further constraints for the managers in that their subordinates were never properly equipped to meet the demands of the workload. This meant that the German middle managers were not allowed to break free from their involvement in the technical tasks, even if they wanted to do so.

> It would be nice to have more time for more intensive and comprehensive employee orientation. If I could do that, things might be easier. As things are, I mainly have to delegate that responsibility for training. Not that I do not trust my subordinates, it is just that not everyone has the complete overview. (Administration Manager, German brewery)

The difference in staff numbers was partly attributable to the relative economic situations of the two countries mentioned above. In Britain the staff numbers had not yet fallen to reflect the slump in business activity, while in Germany they had not caught up with the increase/boom. As one of the Office Managers in the German insurance company put it:

> The main problem is that the number of cases has increased at such a rate that we have reached a point where we have fewer qualified employees than necessary.

But even allowing for these differing economic fortunes, the German companies had at least one and sometimes two fewer tiers of hierarchy than the British companies. What this meant was that there was less cover in the German companies when holes appeared in the fabric of skills. As the accounting manager in the German brewery put it:

> The biggest difficulty is in terms of personnel. For example, the department is quite stretched and we have one employee who has been sick since October. So we have had to make do with

temporary workers. Some of them are good and some are not so good. And anyhow the good ones tend to leave as soon as they master the job because they find something permanent. So it is back to square one. And that is very frustrating, very strenuous.

The lack of personnel not only constrained managers in the way they structured their work; it also established a demand. In order to meet their boss's expectation – that their unit ran smoothly – the German middle managers were forced to get involved in work which should actually have been the responsibility of their subordinates. The German managers observed were regularly required to help out their subordinates when the workload became excessive.

When the volume of work is so great that you cannot catch up to it, you have to make sure that you take some of it away from your employees. (Office Manager, customer services, German insurance company)

Because we do not have enough personnel, I have to take care of too many details on my own. You are always standing with your back to the wall and constantly reacting to events. (Maintenance Manager, German brewery)

Clearly the German middle managers were called upon to act as buffers in a way that their British counterparts were not. Where British managers would tend to negotiate more overtime or to solicit the help of another section, the German managers had to become personally involved. This reflects the fact that German managers are generally better qualified and more temperamentally inclined, than their British counterparts, to get their hands dirty. Furthermore, German middle managers are also regularly assigned technical tasks which they must complete. These, to some extent, offer them the opportunity for choice. This would seem to be corroborated by the fact that the German bosses interviewed found it quite normal that the middle managers should be involved in technical tasks which particularly appealed to them.

As a rule, each section should be run in exactly the same way. But I give the section managers a certain amount of freedom to focus on what they enjoy most and to use their abilities to the full. One is concerned with risk assessment, the other worries more about detailed checking/policing. Each one can choose an area of emphasis out of the technical tasks. (Boss of Claims Processing Managers, German insurance company)

The technical manager can find himself a niche, but he has to discuss it with me and we will consider very closely whether it seems appropriate or not. (Technical director, German construction company)

In the British firms there was little evidence of the middle managers providing the same sort of 'buffer function' as in the German firms. Partly this was due to the higher number of employees and the extra hierarchical levels in British firms which meant that extra work was more easily absorbed lower down the organization. But one also had the impression that, with one exception amongst those studied, the British managers would very rarely see it as appropriate to work on the same tasks as their subordinates.

It transpired that unusual conditions in the economic environment, whatever they happen to be, led to altered work situations for middle managers. Managerial jobs changed over time, not just as a result of negotiation between jobholder and role-senders, but also in ways which may have been outside the control of the jobholder.

Organizational Constraints

Besides the economic context, the more immediate organizational context was considered by some managers to be constraining.

The British managers tended to be especially conscious of organizational constraints. The middle managers in all three British companies were both more critical and more explicit than their German counterparts about what organizational factors inhibited their effectiveness.

Some of the factors cited relate back to demands mentioned previously. For instance, several of the British managers referred to the lack of discretion in the way they could use their budgets. Many also referred to the excessive number of meetings and the fact that they were poorly organized or chaired. Others pointed out inadequacies in the organizational structure resulting in poor communication between the sections.

In addition to these recurrent themes there were more isolated complaints. These ranged from the way open-plan offices caused fragmentation of work-patterns to the problems with control systems or computers; from the constant shifting of goalposts to the frustrations of red tape or internal politics. These examples do not warrant elaboration as they were not cited by enough managers to make them representative. What *is* interesting, is that all the British middle managers perceived distinct constraints in the way they worked.

By contrast, the German middle managers did not seem to perceive many organizational constraints. About the only recurrent one was that associated with bureaucratic office procedures, which corresponded to the British annoyance with red tape:

One thing I do not like is the lengthy decision-making process. Like when I want to initiate something, I do not just have to clear it with one person, but with the whole corporation. When you have ideas and you are ambitious, that can be frustrating. But I suppose that is the way it has to be. If everyone had a new idea every day, it would be complete chaos the next day. There obviously has to be a certain framework and, at times, it is bound to cause paralysis. (Project Manager, German construction company)

What I find frustrating is the lack of influence in certain areas. There are a lot of things that I have to do in a particular way which I would like to do in another way, but which I cannot change. Of course, that is even more frustrating when you later find out that your way of doing it would have worked better. (Regional Administration Manager, German insurance company)

Notwithstanding this bureaucratic impediment, the German middle managers perceived themselves as relatively unconstrained in the way they went about their work. Indeed, several of them considered the freedom in their jobs to be a major source of satisfaction in their jobs.

This perceived freedom seems odd in view of the formal controlling systems, organizational routines and programmes, which were in operation in all three German firms studied. So is there any way of explaining this apparent disparity between perceptions and 'reality' of organizational constraints for both sets of managers?

One possible explanation has to do with the different expectations of middle managers in the two countries. In Britain there is more emphasis on the middle manager acting as a change agent. British middle managers are expected to take initiatives and to turn situations around, to implement ideas of their own and to act in an entrepreneurial fashion. This role inevitably brings them more into contact with the limits of what is possible in the organization. They are therefore more acutely aware of what prevents them from fulfilling that role.

That expectation/characteristic is reinforced by the British emphasis on fitting the job to the person. If managers are told that the job is what they make it, then they will try to shape it to their strengths and preferences, and will occasionally come up against unyielding boundaries.

The German middle managers have a great amount of freedom as long as their decisions, agendas and ideas are compatible with the fairly rigid structural limits of the organization and the expectations of their superiors. The fact that they are very much in tune with the job, in qualifications, technical experience and corporate socialization, means that they are less likely to try things which they know are not possible. It is only on the rare instances when they try to implement their own ideas or objectives – something that requires an alteration in the control systems or which threatens major change – that the limits of their ability to get things done become evident. Thus, more freedom is perceived than actually exists.

CHOOSING WHERE TO GET INVOLVED

Choices are the activities that the jobholder can, but does not have to, do. They are opportunities for one jobholder to do different work from another and to do it in different ways.[4] This simple description does not show that demands, constraints and choices can overlap. Delegation is a good example: what a middle manager may perceive to be a demand of the job may really be choice, since it is a task which he or she has chosen to do rather than delegating it to subordinates. Some tasks, of course, cannot be delegated, but often there is a choice. Conversely, what one manager sees to be an immovable constraint another may consider merely an obstacle to be circumvented. Despite these qualifications as to what really is a choice, there are three reasons why a section on choices should be included. First, because the middle managers studied in both countries did perceive options in what they did and how they did it. Second, because it seems necessary to show the choices that exist in spite of the established demands and organizational and environmental constraints with which middle managers are faced. Third, the British and German managers seem to differ in their perception of these choices.

One of the British managers in the construction company expressed his awareness of choice in jobs in a way that is echoed by many British managers, 'A job is what you make it'. And a British insurance manager enjoyed, 'the responsibility. I am given a fair amount of autonomy by my director . . .'.

In contrast to these rather general expressions of choice by British middle managers are the more specific statements of German middle managers:

Although there are guidelines in terms of organization and legislation you can work fairly independently within these. (Payroll Manager, German brewery).

There is a large amount of autonomy – of course, there are organizational limits, but they are fairly broad. (Commercial Branch Manager, German construction company)

For me it is important to be the master of myself, that is to work the way I like, not to feel my boss standing behind me giving instructions. That is what I enjoy very much in my job. (Customer Services Manager, German insurance company)

The opportunity to choose how to perform the required tasks seemed to be a crucial issue for the middle managers' wellbeing in their working situation in both countries, although these opportunities differed in form and scope. Obviously the British middle managers had a larger amount of choice than their German counterparts because their roles were more open to negotiation. In Germany there were routines that left the managers few opportunities of choosing how to respond to the demands upon them.

The amount of choice varies between the different industries and functions that we studied. In production-oriented functions in brewing and insurance most of the tasks were prescribed by technology or at least by routines which could hardly be circumvented. In the construction industry the middle managers had more choice in how to do the job because the project-orientation of this industry leaves the middle managers a fair amount of autonomy to design the project for which they are responsible. We shall come back to this in Chapter 6, when discussing how structure and technology influence middle managers' roles and behaviour.

Why did our German middle managers perceive choices in their jobs despite being largely constrained by technology or organizational routines? The explanation seems to be that for most their bosses' personal checking was replaced by impersonal means, such as planning procedures and automated checks of results, or by technology, as in the customer service department in the insurance industry or the packaging process in the brewery. The middle managers seemed to see such impersonal checking as less of a constraint upon their autonomy than personal control by their bosses would be, even if, objectively, the scope of choices was limited. Broadly, the same kind of checking applied to the middle managers was adopted by them in checking their subordinates. An exception was the packaging manager in the German brewery who made frequent tours of the shop floor.

The British middle managers, used personal rather than computer checking, probably because organizational routines were far less usual as a means of coordination than in Germany. In their meetings, for instance, they asked the members of their management team to report on processes and results. These meetings, therefore, were not only a means of coordinating the work process but also of checking personally how tasks are performed.

Only when seeking to implement their own ideas or to make changes in work organization and processes did the German managers actually perceive the limitations of their choices. This was particularly true if implementation required changes in technology or routines, which went beyond the middle managers' discretion. In this respect the British middle managers seemed to be better off. They could change work organization in their department as well as decide on the application of technology within their budget and broad company rules. The same patterns showed up in all three industries in the study.

Middle managers in both countries had some choice as to the fragmentation of their working day; how much, depended upon the type of contact. Contacts with superiors, peers or external contacts offered less choice than those with subordinates. When called by their boss, middle managers in both countries interrupted their current work in order to meet his (they were all men) expectations. The same applied to contacts with important customers. The middle managers could, at least to some extent, decide how often, when and under what circumstances subordinates could see them. Some of the British managers signalled their desire to be left undisturbed by closing their door.

The element of choice in contact with subordinates shows in the contact patterns of the four customer service department managers in the German insurance company, all performing the same job. Both the number of contacts with subordinates and the time devoted differed considerably among the four managers observed: from 18 to 99 contacts on a single working day, or from 7 per cent to 35 per cent of working time; nor was there any unusual reason to explain this variation. However, there were limits on the extent to which they could exercise this choice, as their boss pointed out:

> He could perform his job differently in terms of dealing with people. But if his way to deal with subordinates differs significantly, I would intervene and inhibit it. (Head of Customer Services, German insurance company)

The German middle managers had a choice as to which technical tasks they chose not to delegate. Typically the tasks not delegated were those they enjoyed or at which they felt especially competent. Few of the British middle managers had this choice either because of their lack of technical skills or because they did not see such work as appropriate for someone in their position.

For the German middle managers, being able to choose to do some technical tasks could be regarded as a non-monetary incentive, which makes the complex job of a middle manager, with all its stresses, more attractive.

Middle managers in both countries and in all three industries mentioned some tasks that they could delegate, but which they deliberately performed themselves because they saw them as central to their job or department or because their own performance evaluation was based on them:

> If you perform the tasks yourself, you know what is going on and you can fully rely on there being no mistakes. (Packaging Manager, German brewery)

> If I had someone whom I could be totally sure would perform the tasks as well as I do, then I would delegate them at once. (Commercial Branch Manager, German construction company)

These examples do not apply only to German middle managers although they are biased towards technical tasks. In the British brewery, for instance, managers mentioned that they could not delegate tasks because their subordinates were not trained up, so that they themselves had to perform certain tasks, though this was more on the managerial side of their job.

In the British insurance company the managers in the customers service department chose not to delegate those complaints which could be damaging to the company.

The British construction managers performed tasks themselves where status was important, such as, in delicate relations with the client or the design team.

Understanding these choices for middle managers becomes clear if the expectations of their bosses are considered. Though it may have been expressed in a rather vague manner the bosses expected their middle managers to take care of the departments and to run them smoothly. Thus, being involved in those tasks which were critical to the department's performance could be regarded as a demand rather than a choice, since if something went wrong with these the middle manager would be blamed.

In Britain, however, middle managers did not, as a rule, take on technical tasks to facilitate the smooth running of their department. They considered it to be their job as manager to develop their subordinates to do these tasks.

Considerable differences between British and German middle managers could be found in their choice of priorities. In Germany these were nearly all driven by either organizational or environmental incidents. In Britain they were more likely to be motivated by enlighted self-interest, notably in the brewery. For instance, the Distribution Manager was encouraging his computing colleague to look into a cost-saving computing system. Similarly, the Administration and Finance Manager was secretly working on figures to show his boss about the merits of taking on the computing burden themselves rather than paying the centre to do it. These personal priorities coincided with the objectives of the company, but they were being conducted in semi-secret in order to impress their bosses. The idea for middle managers was to always to 'have something up their sleeves'.

A rather strange example of choices was found with German middle managers' attitude to working time. In contrast to their British colleagues they did not make use of their managerial prerogative to choose when to work but rather kept the ordinary office hours in order to demonstrate good practice. Some of them even chose to 'clock in' even though they were not required to do so. One of the construction managers expressed his view as follows:

> I do not want to have prerogatives because I am a manager. I have the same rights and the same duties as everybody else.

In Britain, the middle managers made extensive use of their right to choose the time they were working. This went from starting late in the morning to expanded lunch breaks but also to working rather late in the evening.

SUMMARY

The main similarities between the British and German middle managers were the common demand to run their department smoothly. Both, too, saw good people management and achieving a good working climate in their department as being part of that overall demand. An additional demand on the British managers was the budgetary process, since they, unlike the Germans, had their own departmental budget.

The German managers were more constrained by organizational routines and formal systems, but because these were impersonal, and not personal checking by their boss, they still felt that they had choice. They felt the sense of freedom that comes from knowing the area within which one can operate.

The German managers also felt constrained by a shortage of staff (they had significantly fewer staff than the British managers) and the need to help their overworked subordinates with their tasks. They also, surprisingly, complained more of their staff being inadequately qualified.

The organization of the German companies was more integrated. In the British companies tasks were more broken into separate functions, which made for a greater need for cooperation and a greater danger that objectives could differ. The British managers had to spend more time on securing cooperation.

The British managers had more choice to shape their own job by negotiating their role. They were expected to exercise more initiative and hence were more likely to run into frustrating organizational constraints.

The Germans clocked in to set a good example. The British believed that as managers they had more freedom in when they worked, which could mean starting late and working late.

The British and German managers differed in their choice of priorities. The German managers expected to do technical work, and one of their choices was which technical tasks they did themselves. The British managers made a sharper distinction between their managerial and technical work.

5 What Middle Managers Do

This chapter has two aims: first, to establish those tasks and functions which characterize middle-management work (as distinct from top-management work); and second, to highlight differences between British and German middle managers in how that work is done.

THE DISTINCTIVENESS OF MIDDLE MANAGEMENT

Books about managers have conventionally been about top managers, at least implicitly. The attention of writers and researchers, particularly in the USA and the UK is irresistibly drawn to the corporate boardrooms, towards the change-makers, the high-flyers and peak performers.

Middle management, often by default, is simply assumed to be a scaled-down version of top management. There has been very little attempt to identify what may be qualitatively different about the work of middle managers. The research has only gone as far as to try to establish quantitative differences in the work of senior and middle managers, such as the time-scale of decisions or concerns. As Torrington, Weightman and Johns see it:

> The job of the manager is typically described in terms of the job of the chief executive delegated in different-sized parcels to others and therefore similar to his.[1]

Yet, our research has revealed a number of differences in the role, work patterns and activities of middle managers compared to senior managers. In other words, *what* middle managers do, *how* they do it and *where* they do it, is in many ways different from what we already know about their senior colleagues from other studies. The aim in this first section is to highlight those middle-management characteristics that are consistent across both countries.

Underpinning the distinctiveness of middle-management work is its pivotal role. It is at the juncture – up, down and across – of everything that is given and received in the organization: information, instructions, explanations, advice, ideas and expectations. It is responsible for reconciling conflicting objectives, securing cooperation, interpreting plans, and implementing decisions.

Middle management therefore serves a buffer function. The role of middle managers is to ensure the smooth running of their section or to 'keep the show on the road'.[2] They are expected to create an effective working environment, to neutralize any factors, whether social or technical, that might impede the portion of the work process for which they are responsible. That means resolving difficulties within the section as well as minimizing harmful influences from above or from adjacent sections. It involves middle managers in both preventive and reactive measures.

In layman's terms, this role can best be described as one of 'holding it together' as coined by Haire some 35 years ago:

It seems strange to me that the function of holding the organization together is not more heavily weighted in job descriptions of executives. Usually we read that they collect information, make decisions, see that decisions are carried out, and the like. Observing executive behaviour it seems to me that most time and effort is spent in holding the thing together as a single working unit.[3]

In discharging this role, both sets of middle managers observed had many activities in common. First and foremost, there was the heavy emphasis on giving, gathering and piecing together information from various quarters. Our middle managers spent the vast majority of their time handling information, asking questions and using their powers of observation. This provided clues as to who was and who was not performing well, where problems might have arisen, how they and their sections were perceived from above. For middle managers it was important to get a feel for what was going on around them. The more accurate the picture, the better they could do their jobs. They were dealers in information. As Horne and Lupton observed in a study in 1965 of middle management, which anticipated many of our own findings:

Overwhelmingly the largest slice of total time of managers is spent dealing with information, mainly in giving, receiving and seeking it. The phone calls, the face-to-face meetings, the discussion groupings, and the formal meetings which occupy so much time seem to serve to a large extent to pass information, and perhaps to seek, give, or compare explanations.[4]

Thus, for all the rhetoric about empowerment and acting as change agents, middle management is still about working within an environment rather than shaping that environment. As one of the managers observed put it: 'The choices in my job are to do with *how* I do things, not so much *what* I do.' Again, Horne and Lupton confirm this view of middle management:

> Managers talk most of the time, and mostly face-to-face. They seem not to be overwhelmed with paper or formal meetings. They swop information and advice and instructions, mostly through informal face to face contact in their own offices. Middle management does not seem, on this showing, to require the exercise of remarkable powers to analyse, weigh alternatives, and decide. Rather, it calls for the ability to shape and utilize the person-to-person channels of communication, to influence, to persuade, to facilitate.[5]

The work of middle managers, then, differed from that of their bosses in the amount of control they had over it. They were not originators but interpreters. Theirs was not to formulate but to decide how to go about reaching given objectives. As Horne and Lupton put it:

> Middle managers spend much more of their time facilitating, manipulating, and regulating than they do deciding about objectives, policies and plans.[6]

It follows that the greatest skill required by middle managers was the ability to implement what was planned by others, to translate the strategic into the workable. They operated within a framework which they could easily change.

A great deal of the middle managers' time in both countries was, as will be shown on the following pages, simply spent checking and cross-checking – face to face, over the phone, from reports and print-outs, in scheduled meetings and in *ad hoc* exchanges. Although the two sets of managers went about the checking in different ways and checked different things, the activity itself was constant. They were checking on the successful resolution of past problems and checking that things were in place to avoid future problems.

Middle managers also differed from top managers in their range of contacts. To start with, our middle managers on average had only a few external contacts. But they did, by definition, have to deal upwards, as well as downwards and laterally. They therefore had to 'manage' their own and other people's bosses, as well as handle colleagues over whom they had no authority. While top managers mainly dealt with other managers, middle managers also had to deal with, and be sensitive to the expectations and requirements of non-managerial staff.

In particular, middle managers were charged with developing their staff. In both countries this meant helping them learn organizational routines and problem-solving tasks. Middle managers were well-placed to do this for, as repositories of the corporate memory, it was they who represented the continuity and values of the company. To perform this corporate service effectively, however, middle managers had to put their own interests to the side. In Britain they had a wider development role. They were expected to nurture talent in the full knowledge that the quicker it happened, the more quickly they would be deprived of it; with the added blow that those they brought on might soon rise above them in the organization.

Besides what they did, and whom they did it with, middle managers also differed from senior managers in *where* they did it. Formal meetings aside, over 90 per cent of the working day was generally spent in the manager's own office – for British and German managers alike. The rest of the time was spent mainly in activities elsewhere in the company premises. Thus, the middle managers spent most of their time not just in their own companies, but in their own offices – this in spite of the academic emphasis on, and legitimization of, 'management by walking around'. In our study there were few exceptions to this. These exceptions could be traced back to the particular responsibilities of the jobholders. Thus, the managers studied in the German construction firm were more likely to spend time outside the company, because of their technical tasks, just as the sales managers in the German brewery spent a great deal of their workday on activities outside the organization.

All this pointed to a stark difference between top and middle managers. The former were concerned with shaping, the latter with holding together. Top managers tried to define objectives and devise initiatives, while middle managers were charged with creating and maintaining the conditions in which effective implementation could take place. These are differences which have an impact on outlook and consciousness, as well as the skills required.

Having established that middle management represented a discrete layer of management with its own set of demands, choices and constraints, we can now explore how British and German managers differed in their approach to their work.

MAINLY TALKING AND LISTENING

What the middle managers did most was to talk and listen. Table 5.1 shows the percentage of working time where there was no contact. In other words, it shows those periods of observation when the managers were alone either reading, writing or using a computer.

On twenty-one of the thirty-two observation days, the fourteen British middle managers spent less than 20 per cent of their time alone. For the thirteen German managers, only nine of their twenty-nine observation days involved less than 20 per cent of their time alone.

At the other end of the scale, there were only three instances (out of 32) of the British managers spending more than 40 per cent of their working day in isolation – and none over 50 per cent. In contrast, the German managers spent over 40 per cent of their time alone on eleven of the twenty-nine observation days – with one manager achieving a startling 83 per cent on one day.

There were also considerable differences between managers from different firms within one country, which indicated that there were other influences apart from cross-cultural differences shaping the amount of time spent talking and listening. The German middle managers, especially, differed enormously in the time spent alone with a range from 4.8 per cent to 83.3 per cent.

A comparison of the three German companies shows that the managers in the construction firm consistently interacted the most while those in the insurance firm interacted the least. This was because of the different cooperation requirements assigned to the middle managers' positions (see Chapter 4). The fairly standardized

Table 5.1   Time spent alone

% of working day spent alone	British managers	German managers
Average	19.9	36.5
Maximum Number	47.1	83.3
Minimum Number	0	4.8

products of the insurance company facilitated a far-reaching structuring of work-processes in the form of organizational rules and standards. The need for collaboration between the departments in the German insurance firm could, therefore, be reduced to a minimum. By contrast, the buyer market in the German construction industry, and the uncertainties associated with each different construction project, prevented a structuring of the work-processes and the use of technocratic coordination instruments. Personal cooperation, which met the demands of individual projects, became a central instrument in the coordination of the work-processes.

Comparing the three pairs of companies, it was the German and British insurance firms that differed most from each other. The middle managers in the British insurance company relied far more on verbal communication than did their German counterparts. Partly this was a result of the way that the work was structured, as we shall show in Chapter 6.

Meetings

As with time spent alone, the time that managers spent in meetings was easy to measure and classify. This varied considerably between industries and functions, as well as between the two countries.

For instance, in the breweries there was a marked difference between the managers directly involved with the production process and those who were not. In both the British and the German breweries, the 'line' managers all held daily progress meetings, lasting somewhere between 15 and 30 minutes. These involved the head of function and the shift manager, together with their counterparts from the maintenance department. The aim of these meetings was to coordinate maintenance and production activities.

While the purpose of this meeting was the same in both countries, the contents and tone of the meeting differed somewhat. For instance, in the German brewery, the problems were primarily technically driven, for example, working out at what time of the day specific equipment should be serviced or perhaps discussing the quality of maintenance provision. British meetings also had such technical subjects, but industrial relations and personnel issues also impinged heavily.

In both countries, for those managers not directly involved in producing or distributing the beer, meetings tended to be longer but far less frequent. The meetings involved briefing information downwards and controlling the work of subordinates, or else they were review-type meetings, where they would get together with colleagues and/or bosses to audit past events, and discuss future events.

In the construction industry, a somewhat different pattern emerged. It is in the nature of project work to progress through meetings. Thus all the managers observed in both countries, were heavily involved in meetings. Most of the meetings observed were project-driven, particularly to do with the tender process and the practicalities of setting-up or closing projects. The preparation, coordination, controlling and checking (monitoring financial and technical progress, and scheduling) of the construction projects mostly took place in the regional office. There were also various reporting meetings. In the British construction company these ranged from monthly profit- and loss-reviews, site audits and site-audit presentations (to boss), to fortnightly strategy meetings and production meetings. Current and completed contracts were also reviewed on a weekly or monthly basis. Once a week, the commercial and technical managers visited the sites for which they were responsible in order to make a more detailed appraisal of progress. Site meetings with the client's representative and the architect were held monthly. In Germany a similar pattern of meetings was found. But what was different was that the commercial managers did not visit the sites regularly.

The sector where there was the widest disparity in meetings between the two countries was insurance. For instance, none of the four German administration managers attended a single scheduled meeting over the eight days of observation. In contrast, their four British counterparts attended a total of four scheduled meetings between them (in eight days), lasting nearly six hours – and judging by the information about meetings given in their questionnaire, this was a light week. The four managers said that they expected to spend an average of between six-and-a-quarter and nine-and-three-quarter hours per week in regular scheduled meetings (see Table 5.2).

On top of these scheduled meetings, there were also *ad hoc* meetings. Once again, the British insurance managers easily outstripped their German counterparts.

Here too, structural differences were largely accountable for the different meeting requirements. In the German insurance company, there was an integrated approach to handling policies. In other words, each customer service department was set up to handle any sort of query from a given policy-holder, from underwriting and altering insurance policies to paying out on claims (see previous

Table 5.2 Average time spent in scheduled meetings per week for the customer service managers in the British insurance company

Function	Average number of hours per week*
Alterations Manager	7h15
Quality Control Manager	9h45
New Business Manager	7h50
Renewals Manager	6h15
Technical Services Manager	8h35

* This figure is calculated by taking the duration and frequency of regular scheduled meetings for the year and dividing by the number of working weeks.

chapter for more details about differences in meetings and the reasons for them).

Besides the obligatory coordination or communication meetings, the British insurance managers were involved in steering committees and project groups. Many of the British managers also became involved in open-ended forums with staff. The boss of the middle managers, for instance, met each of them one-to-one, for an hour every week, simply to discuss progress.

On top of the time actually spent in the meetings, time was spent in meeting-related activities – preparation time (agendas, information, notes, and tactics in one case), and discussion between the participants of how the meeting went, of particular issues that arose, and one-to-one communication of critical feedback to direct subordinates. This prompted the thought that from the point of view of the British insurance managers, 'the meetings *are* the work'.

This discussion suggests that the number and duration of meetings held by a manager is influenced by four variables: the type of product, the type of job, the organizational structure, and the prevailing culture.

Type of product
The complexity of a company's product and the extent to which it can be standardized have considerable influence on the personal coordination required. The more a company's product is standardized and the less complex it is, the easier it is to replace coordination by personal cooperation by general solutions through rules and

standards, as in the German insurance firm, as described in Chapter 6. Where the product is highly complex and there is little possibility for standardization there is a high need for personal communication. The development of general solutions for the coordination of work processes is more difficult and may even be impossible.

Type of job

For example, line jobs in production departments using a process technology seem to require shorter, more regular (and more reactive) meetings. In the two breweries, for instance, the line jobs required coordination with maintenance on a daily basis (30 minutes per day).

The service functions – notably the brewery payroll manager – could sometimes manage without scheduled meetings; or could space out their meetings over longer periods. For example, in the British construction company, the quality manager had to carry out quality audits and his whole job was to visit sites, subcontractors and suppliers. But it was up to him when he did this.

Organizational level also had some bearing on the need to attend meetings. While the British middle managers were involved in more meetings than their German counterparts, their days were not dominated by meetings in the same way as in Mintzberg's study of five American chief executives who spent an average of 59 per cent of their working day in meetings. This is to be expected since movement up the hierarchy is accompanied by less 'hands-on' activity. It would suggest that involvement in meetings is a hierarchical variable too.

Organizational structure

This has a strong impact on the incidence of meetings. For instance, none of the German companies had a separate quality function which launched initiatives, conducted audits or impinged on managerial time. Similarly, in the German insurance industry, there was no separate technical support or business requirements group, which are the service equivalent of the maintenance function in manufacturing companies.

These structural factors meant that British managers engaged in more routine coordination – laterally and vertically. On only four out of thirty-two observation days, British managers spent less than 10 per cent of their time in meetings. In contrast, the German managers spent less than ten per cent of their time in meetings on twelve out of twenty-nine observation days.

British companies often also differed from German companies in having grown by acquisition or through divisionalization: this prompted an additional need for 'cross-over meetings' between different parts of the group. All three British case-studies required some of their managers to take part in steering committees, working parties, project groups or liaison meetings of some kind. For instance, the new business manager in the UK insurance company, spent two hours a week with the management team and two hours a week with his own team – in addition he had to attend seven separate liaison meetings ranging from 30 minutes to two hours duration.

Such activities were much less important for the German middle managers. But even some of the German middle managers took part in meetings which were concerned with the coordination of projects or the integration of newly acquired companies.

Prevailing culture

Organizational and national culture also have an impact on the incidence and duration of meetings. For instance, British managers, who were less time- and task-conscious than German ones, were more likely to tolerate prolonged meetings. Setting aside daily briefings lasting about thirty minutes, first thing in the morning, one-and-a-half to two hours seemed to be the norm for open-ended type meetings in the British companies – and a number of the meetings were simply pencilled in for 'the morning' or 'the afternoon'.

One of the reasons for this British view of meetings was that they were perceived as being places where wider information is picked up, impressions are formed and ideas are floated. Meetings were more likely to be regarded as important 'clearing houses' for soft information, and also as places where inexperienced managers learn to take a broader view. Meetings, in Britain, play a role which goes beyond the process of communication, coordination, problem-resolution and decision-making. They may also be perceived as serving a motivational and developmental function.

In German firms – judging by the impressions formed during the observations – noticeably more weight was placed upon technical subjects having to do with the departments and less upon a more general exchange of information. Furthermore, the German middle managers made a point of keeping the meetings as brief as possible. This effort was reflected in certain routines which could frequently be observed during the meetings. The participants of a meeting each presented their problems, concerns or plans and only those participants who were directly affected by the problem made comments, while the others exercised disciplined restraint.

But within each country, there were also differences: the British insurance company was clearly more meetings-oriented than the brewery. Partly this was institutionalized in the obligatory review processes, but it was also promoted through the use of 'coffee mornings' and 'awaydays' for units – a lead which came strongly from the top. Similarly, the German insurance company was clearly less partial to meetings than the brewery or the construction company.

Ad Hoc Interaction

When they were neither alone nor in meetings, the managers were involved in *ad hoc* interaction, either over the phone or face to face. These telephone conversations, informal exchanges, inquiries or requests accounted for the largest portion of their time.

The German managers made slightly more use of the telephone than did their British counterparts: an average of twenty-four calls per day compared with the British managers' seventeen. However, the telephone conversations of the German middle managers were, on average, shorter, averaging two minutes, than those of the British managers observed, which averaged three minutes.

More important than the fairly small difference in the number of calls, the British managers made *qualitatively* different use of the phone. They were particularly inclined to use the phone to exchange information that was not task-related, to form impressions, and to engage in speculation. On the continuum which runs 'task-related – political – speculation – gossip – private', British managers were far more likely than their German counterparts to stray out of the first category. This point is developed later in this chapter (under the heading 'Enlisting cooperation').

The German managers had far more *ad hoc* contacts than their British counterparts as shown in Table 5.3, and a very wide spread between maximum and minimum.

Table 5.4 shows that the British managers' *ad hoc* contacts took longer, so that they actually spent more time with *ad hoc* contacts than did the German managers with their more frequent contacts. One possible explanation lies in their different views of management. For the British managers, management was a hands-off activity. Direct involvement in the work of subordinates was to be avoided since it was considered to stifle the development of subordinates and

Table 5.3 Number of *ad hoc* contacts for both sets of middle managers observed

Number of ad-hoc contacts per day	British managers	German managers
Average	33	52
Maximum Number	75	137
Minimum Number	14	4

Table 5.4 Percentage of working day taken up by *ad hoc* contacts

% of day taken up by ad-hoc contact	British managers	German managers
Average	33.6	27.2
Maximum Number	53.9	47
Minimum Number	4.9	3.6

to distract the manager from higher order priorities (see also later section entitled 'Understanding of management'). Thus, when British managers talked to their subordinates, it was not about the technicalities of their work, but about their work in more general terms. They monitored progress in a more roundabout way which, inevitably, took more time. Their role was to oversee and motivate.

The German managers conveyed the picture that they had risen to their position by virtue of their superior technical knowledge. They saw themselves as repositories of experience and know-how on which their subordinates could draw. They motivated and led their subordinates by example. They *did* get involved in the work of their subordinates, either through detailed checking, or else simply by being available for technical inquiries. It follows that their contact with subordinates tended to be short and to the point – a technical query answered – since many of them relied primarily on detailed checking of the output of the section. But this does not fully explain the considerable differences between managers in the number of *ad hoc* contacts and the share of time they took up. To do this we must consider the context of the job.

Exchanges with subordinates were the most common informal interaction and took up the greatest share of middle-management time. This was true for British and German middle managers alike. The German middle managers had a daily average of fifty-seven contacts with their employees, which represented about 55 per cent of their verbal interaction at work. Behind these average figures there were big differences in the amount of interaction depending on the job and the context. At the low end were the office managers in the German insurance company who spent an average of one and a half minutes with each contact. This brevity of contact can be ascribed to the extensive standardization of the technical tasks of the insurance agents as well as the middle managers. Middle managers dealing with technical tasks in the German construction firm had relatively fewer contacts than the middle managers in the insurance firm, but these contacts were considerably longer. This can be explained by the low possibility of standardizing subordinates' tasks. For instance, analysing problems of individual construction projects as well as developing or communicating solutions to problems took up more time than the standardized problem-solving steps at the insurance firm. Communication episodes with colleagues were less frequent, but tended to last longer than contacts with subordinates.

Here again the considerable differences that were found between the middle managers observed in the German companies could be traced back to the various contextual factors of different positions. Because of the small need for personal cooperation, the share of horizontal verbal communication of the total time spent on communication of the observed middle managers in the customer service department of the insurance firm was 10 per cent, whereas the middle managers in the construction firm had a share of 22 per cent. Given that the verbal communication of the middle managers in the customer service department of the insurance firm took up less than 40 per cent of the workday, while that of the managers in the construction firm took up more than 75 per cent, the absolute differences in the amounts of horizontal communication are even more striking.

Contact with the boss was fairly unusual outside structured situations. In the German firms, informal contact with the boss was consistently rare and brief. In the British context, it varied somewhat but seemed largely to depend on personal empathy rather than actual needs. The most striking example was in the British brewery where the distribution director (boss of the distribution manager) would often come to his subordinate's office for coffee and a chat, before the official 8.30 a.m. start. These daily gatherings, lasting between twenty and thirty minutes, were informal but important forums, generally involving three layers of hierarchy (the distribution manager, his two subordinates and his boss). The discussion switched easily from social chit-chat (holidays, gossip) to medium and even long-term problems within the distribution department. They speculated about the future of the telephone sales function – whether it would be integrated into sales; the future of the cost-cutting computer programme; the relevance of night-trunking; the checkers' problem and voluntary redundancies. Problems, ranging from the human to the technical to the strategic were communicated up and down, and kicked around.

Notwithstanding the three or four British managers who had regular informal contact with their bosses, this was not the norm. It would be true to say that in both countries, contact with superiors occurred mostly during structured meetings where others, particularly colleagues of the middle manager, were present.

These findings are very much in line with Stewart's previous findings regarding contact time with boss and subordinates. Stewart's 1967 study revealed that managers varied widely in the time spent with their boss,[7] ranging from zero to over 20 per cent of their working time, the mean being 8 per cent. Immediate subordinates took up more than twice as much of the managers' time on average than any other contact.[8]

MULTITUDE OF ACTIVITIES

Our sample of middle managers in Germany and Britain had a multitude of activities during the workday: an average of 121 a day for the Germans and 77 for the British. An overview is presented in Table 5.5.

Despite the multitude of activities recorded during our observations, we question whether this can be called fragmentation, as most of the previous studies on managers' work activities have done. A closer look at the observation data suggests that what has been called managers' 'fragmented working day' is, at least in some jobs, a methodological artifact which arises where no attention is paid to the contents of a manager's activities or to the processual links between individual activities. This can be illustrated by two examples.

Table 5.5 Type and number of work activities for middle managers
observed in Germany and Britain

Type of activity	British middle managers			German middle managers		
	average number	average duration in min.	% of working time	average number	average duration in min.	% of working time
Desk work	21	5	19.8	40	4	36.5
Telephone	17	3	9.3	24	2	12.8
Scheduled meetings	1	67	10.0	1	42	6.7
Unscheduled meetings	2	64	20.2	3	21	14.5
Further contacts	33	6	33.6	52	2	27.2
Other	3	13	7.1	1	20	2.3

Example 5.1   German Insurance Company

All but one of the middle managers observed in the customer
service department had more than 130 daily activities. They were
obliged to check the work of their subordinates if the sums
insured were over a certain amount and, if appropriate, release
that money for payment. Because of the high level of standardization of the employee's work, cases which required evaluation
could usually be checked very quickly. This meant that, within a
period of, say ten minutes, where an office manager was alone at
his desk, a large amount of work could be *individually* checked
without noticeably affecting the activity criteria and, therefore,
providing no measurable amount of fragmentation. If the
managers started a new activity, such as a discussion with a
subordinate or a telephone call, after he had finished checking
the work of his employees, then fragmentation was measured,
even if – and this is important – the manager had not interrupted
or had not been interrupted in his work. Fragmentation in this
case was not real but the result of a coding method, which
equated number of activities with the amount of fragmentation.

Example 5.2   German Construction

It also became clear with the middle managers here that more fragmentation was measured than actually occured. Thus, during a meeting with his subordinates, one of the managers observed completed activities belonging to different specified activity classifications, while the contents of these activities were directly associated with the subjects discussed at the meeting. He frequently interrupted meetings to give instructions, to pass on important information he learned at the meeting or to use the telephone to obtain further information needed for the meeting. These examples show the need to be more careful about equating the number of activities with fragmentation, because the contents of a manager's activities are often closely related.

AGENDAS

The concept of agendas and networks, developed by John Kotter,[9] provides a useful way of trying to understand what managers are seeking to achieve. As Kotter sees it, agendas are mental representations of the manager's mixed goals relating to his or her job responsibilities. His concept of agenda enables an observer to view the manager's activities as a process directed towards achieving the agenda rather than as isolated occurrences.

Managers can only progress towards their goals with the help of others. Thus, Kotter described how the general managers he studied built up networks of people within and outside the organization who could help them to execute their agendas.

Kotter developed the concept of 'agenda' when he was studying general managers whose tasks and responsibilities were, compared with middle managers, unstandardized and unstructured. Agendas, as Kotter understands them, were not widely used by the middle managers studied and therefore cannot adequately explain their behaviour. One possible reason is that tasks and responsibilities of these middle managers were more structured than those of general managers and embedded within organizational programmes and routines. The relationships needed to fulfil the tasks were also usually well-established and in the British companies could be spelt out in job descriptions. Therefore, neither work agendas nor network-building required much creative input from the middle managers.

Nevertheless many of the middle managers had plans for their areas. Some of those observed had what they referred to as a 'vision' or a 'direction' which they wanted to pursue for their unit, and they saw themselves as having a role, rather than simply doing a job. Evidence of agenda-setting was clearest among the recently rotated British middle managers.

Two extreme examples of agendas of German middle managers are presented below. The first is an example of a short-term pursuit of a task set by the manager's boss. Despite its simplicity it is worth describing as an example of a non-standardized activity, in an otherwise pretty routinized setting, which required the manager to search for ways of achieving the agenda set by the boss. The second is an illustration of a much broader and more personalized agenda which could be pursued in a less structured environment.

Example 5.3

(a) Agenda: Customer Service Manager, German Insurance

08.11.1991

13:50   In a meeting scheduled shortly before, the middle manager who was observed and her colleagues were told by their supervisor that the *Bundesaufsichtsamt für Versicherung* (BAV) (Federal Bureau of Insurance Regulation) then currently auditing the insurance company, requested a description of certain cases. Their supervisor suggested that each office head should concentrate on two cases, and stressed that this task should be completed quickly and further specified that the cases to be presented should not be extreme cases.

Two further activities

14:17   Searches for current assigments within her department which correspond to the above-mentioned cases. Does not find any.
14:21   Goes into a colleague's office to look for cases.

14:23 Returns to her office with a few files and begins to look through them. Is interrupted by an employee.

Two further activities

14:28 Continues studying files, but is interrupted shortly thereafter.

Two further activities

14:35 A subordinate comes with a case for which she is looking, but it does not meet the requirements.
14:36 The files, which she brought from the office of her colleague, also do not meet the requirements. Thereupon, she phones various colleagues and their subordinates (a total of five telephone conversations) to ask about the needed cases and requests them to call back if the assignment is being currently worked on in their department.

One further activity

14:49 Receives a call that one of the sought-after assignments has been found in another department. Goes to her colleague to pick up this assignment and expresses her thanks.

One further activity

14:55 Reads a list in which the needed cases are recorded. Asks a subordinate whether he knows where the cases which are on the list could be found.
14:57 Goes to the filing department to continue looking for the needed cases.
15:05 Searches through the files, telephones a colleague and discusses with him a case she has found in the cabinet. It seems to meet the requirements.
15:07 A colleague phones to say that he has found a sought-after case in his department.

One further activity

15:11   Reads the files which she has brought from the file department.

.13 further activities

15:30   A subordinate of a colleague comes and brings a case with her. She looks through the file. This case seems to meet the requirements too.

Example 5.4

(b) Agenda: Sales Manager,German Brewery

The agenda of this middle manager entails a much greater time-period for achievement than that of the middle manager described above and, because of the relatively brief three-day period of observation, could not be recorded in its entirety.

   During our conversation, the observed manager said that from a meeting with a sales representative of A-Cola, he believes that the brewery's profit margins for the caffeinated drink, B-Cola (which is currently dispensed in restaurants which serve the brewery's beer), are lower than those that could be achieved with A-Cola. In the meantime, he has received related pricing information from A-Cola.

11.09.1991

10:10   The observed middle manager hears his boss's secretary in the hallway. He goes to her and asks for the next possible appointment with his supervisor, who is the member of the board of directors reponsible for marketing.

10:15   Receives a telephone call from the secretary and is given an appointment for that afternoon.

14:00   We were not allowed to observe the meeting that took place with his boss and which lasted 1 hr. 37 min. But the observed manager told us that, in addition to other topics the meeting dealt with the task of raising profit margins by implementing his idea of replacing one product with another.

16:01   He phones a colleague in the calculation department (*Betriebswirtschaftliche Abteilung*) and tells him that he would like to talk to him for ten minutes. Then he briefly informs the colleague about the topic of the conversation, namely that he must prepare a report for the Board of Directors, in which possibilities for raising profit margins are to be presented. He further mentions that he believes that the board has been provided with incorrect figures. A date is set for 13.09.1991.

12.09.1991

Because of the observed middle manager's activities on this day, it is not possible for him to follow this topic on his agenda.

13.09.1991

10:12 He goes to the scheduled meeting with his colleague from the calculation department which lasts for thirty-five minutes. He presents his idea, arguing from a cost point of view and states his supposition that maybe the wrong calculations have been used. His colleague argues against the observed manager's solution (he must, because it was his department that generated the calculations to the previous decision). The observed manager repeats his argument. Then together they look at the actual sales figures of the caffeinated drink, which they currently utilize. The observed manager brings in further arguments, which are not quantifiable. He concedes that perhaps the figures were not wrongly calculated, but that they may need to be calculated in a different manner. His colleague argues that the problem cannot be solved by cost-related arguments and that it would be more worthwhile to present the argument to the board with respect to the actual product, since it is barely selling.

They discuss the potential developments which a product change would cause and what effects it would have on profit margins. The change would also have other advantages which would lead to cost reductions. A-Cola would offer the necessary filling machines. Then possible difficulties are discussed. For instance, who would become the actual partner to the contract, the sales representative of A-Cola or A-Cola itself? Another problem would be if the brewery could simply withdraw from its current contract with B-Cola. The observed manager adds that he is currently meeting with the sales representative, and his colleague informs him who originally was responsible for the contract with the producer of the caffeinated drink, which is currently being purchased by the brewery, and who, therefore, must have the information about the exact terms of the contract. His colleague offers to recalculate everything, but requests that the observed manager is to bring him the further pricing information necessary for the calculations. Both men agree on what further information will be necessary for the presentation, and also to try to find out from sources above (the Board of Directors) what the possibilities are of an acceptance of the project.

The extent to which an agenda has been structured, the scope of the agenda and the extent to which it requires middle managers to complete individual tasks vary considerably. These differences cannot be explained only by a middle manager's personal characteristics. Whether such broad agendas, as observed in the case of the sales manager or the managers in the German construction company, can even be developed by managers in a company depends upon a number of factors, of which a manager's personal ability is only one. The fact that the middle managers observed in the German insurance firm do not have such wide-ranging plans of action can be explained by the fact that their tasks, as well as the work-processes necessary for managing these tasks, are highly standardized and extensively dictated by technology. Solutions to problems do not have to be developed by the jobholder in the form of an agenda; they have already been specified.

Relatively abstract objectives, such as profit or contribution margins, may offer more possibilities for developing individual action plans than do more concrete objectives. But then – and this is a further departure from the circumstances of the general managers observed by Kotter – the decision whether to implement a plan of action is the responsibility of the middle manager's superior, or even of corporate management. This can also be seen in the agenda of the sales manager observed. He developed a plan to raise contribution margins and tried to collect information necessary to the implementation of his agenda through a network of cooperative contacts. But whether his agenda will be fulfilled or not must be decided at the executive level.

Kotter's concept of agendas and their implementation by managers can only be applied under certain conditions to the middle managers we observed. The possibilities for implementing individually developed agendas may not even exist in jobs where the necessary decision-making freedom to implement one's own conceptual ideas or plans, which could be counteracting to higher organizational strategies or goals, is not present. Decision-making freedom may be restricted by senior managers' wish to coordinate the activities of different parts of the company. This became evident in some of the bosses' interviews. As a technical director in the German construction company expressed it:

> The construction manager can choose his niche . . . but we would like to be informed about it and keep an eye on it, whether it is OK or not.

Kotter's concept of agendas, developed in a study of general managers, can provide only a partial explanation of the behaviour of middle managers, even when his fundamental assumption that managerial activities are related to one another by processes is proved correct. The element of planning, which is associated with the concept of agendas, seems often not to be present in the actual work-behaviour of middle managers, or at least not to be easily identified. Instead, many actions of middle managers seem to lie on a continuum between the two extremes of a quasi-automatic action and the conscious execution of an agenda. The explanation may be that middle managers have developed scripts for managing standard situations.

SCRIPTS

A script is a scheme in a person's mind which contains actions or behaviours (or sequences of actions or behaviours) that can be applied in specific contexts or situations.[10] 'Schematic' means that the knowledge of a concrete experience is stored in abstract form. Schemes are understood to be cognitive patterns which allow an individual to structure future social situations and information, to give them meaning and to understand them. Scripts have two important functions. 'They enable the understanding of ongoing organisational events, and they provide a guide to appropriate behaviour.'[11]

Scripts are formed from a collection of experiences, such as those gained through the manager's interaction with other company employees and his or her participation in certain events and situations. Scripts are then enhanced through the repetition of these experiences.

Scripts make it possible for an individual to manage/deal with familiar or stereotypical situations by referring to already-developed problem solutions. This does not mean that the managers do not or cannot think about what they do. They are familiar with the behaviour patterns and sequences to which each situation corresponds and they choose between these behaviour patterns, even when they implement/learn these models more or less subconsciously.

Because of the long time that German middle managers remain in a position, and their slow career climb within one functional area, they often know in detail the problems which could arise in the work and work-processes within their departments as well as the necessary steps to take in solving these problems. They are in the position to react directly to the current situation 'without having to think it over'. The number of such standardized work situations and the extent to which these situations are standardized varies with the contextual factors of a position. These factors determine where the majority of a position holder's actions lie on the continuum – tending toward quasi-automatic behavioural sequences or toward a conscious implementation of agendas. This will again be illustrated with two extreme examples of the typical work situations of German middle managers.

A central demand with which all middle managers are confronted is to make sure that the work and work-processes in their departments run smoothly. They must, particularly in the German companies, be accessible when their subordinates have problems managing tasks and assist in the problem-solving process. (See below under the heading 'Checking and Control' for the difference between the British and German managers' view of subordinates bringing problems.) For the customer services managers in the German insurance company, this type of situation usually takes the following course:

Example 5.5

A subordinate comes with various documents to the office supervisor and begins the contact with an introduction such as: 'I have a problem here' or 'I have a question here' so that the supervisor will know what the conversation will be about. The employee cannot get any further on processing the claim and expects support from the supervisor. The next step of this schematically progressing behaviour sequence is an analysis of the problem. If it is a familiar problem for the supervisor he will tell the subordinate what to do, from the many years of experience, which have been stored in his memory. If the supervisor is not familiar with the necessary problem-solving steps, he contacts a colleague who is viewed as an expert in this problem area. The contact process between the supervisor and his colleague progresses in the same way as that between the subordinate and the manager. After a short greeting, the office supervisor also indicates his expectation through a remark such as: 'We have a problem here.' After the solution is conveyed, it is further passed on to the subordinate.

An important indicator for the very schematic, quasi-automatic character of this behaviour sequence is the time it takes to react to certain situations or certain signals. Thus, an average contact length between a manager and subordinate of only one-and-one-half minutes indicates a high degree of routinization of behaviour of the office manager in the insurance firm.

A large part of the office manager's work day is taken up by such behaviour sequences. That the manager often relies on this scripted behaviour and quasi-automatic course of behaviour sequences can be traced back to the comprehensive structuring and standardization of the subordinate's tasks as well as of the duties of the manager.

Behaviour sequences which can be described as following a script are much less common and less well-developed in the work of the middle managers in the construction industry, because the work is much less standardized. Nevertheless, our observation of the German technical branch manager's consultations with his subordinates showed similar behavioural patterns which can be thought of as following an implicit script:

Example 5.6

The manager's experience will have enabled him to develop an analysis of particular construction projects according to certain topics. Behaviour sequences vary considerably within this structure. The characteristics of the script are weaker than in the insurance industry because the problems are sufficiently different from those in previous situations to make a quasi-automatic scripted procedure impossible. The behaviour sequences of the technical site manager are much more widely distributed across the continuum between agenda and script with some activities being accomplished quasi-automatically, while the majority of activities are accomplished through the conscious use of agendas. It also became clear that, during consultations with subordinates which lasted longer than in the other two companies, methods of solving the particular problem were developed, often with the help of another colleague's expert knowledge.

ENLISTING COOPERATION

Managers cannot do very much by themselves. To get things done they need the cooperation of others – their bosses and colleagues, and above all, their subordinates. From both our observation and interviews, there were marked differences in the way cooperation was solicited in each country.

For the German managers in all three companies, enlisting cooperation was considered a fairly straightforward affair. The question 'How would you go about enlisting cooperation?' prompted variations on the key phrase '*überzeugen mit sachlichen Argumenten*' (convince with factual arguments).

The consistent view among the German middle managers was that the best way to convince others is to argue one's case based on facts stemming from a thorough knowledge of the situation or subject. Technical mastery and an understanding of the contents of subordinates' tasks were repeatedly emphasized; and the key words in the managers' answers were *fachlich* (job/task-related), *wissen* (to know) and *beherrschen* (being able to perform, to master).

As German middle managers saw it *Glaubwürdigkeit* (credibility) and *Fachkenntnis/Fachwissen* (technical knowledge) went hand in hand. Senior managers who became *fachlich* (remote) and who no longer seemed to understand what happened on the shop floor, quickly lost credibility.

From the observation, there was usually little convincing of middle managers required from senior managers to implement changes or to push through decisions. It would be assumed by those on the receiving end that the necessary staff work had taken place, which had allowed the senior managers to make a well-considered decision based on facts. Senior managers' decisions were rarely questioned, and if they were, it would constitute a considerable criticism of their managerial abilities.

As the German managers saw it, facts and rational arguments are the means of persuasion. Attempts to persuade others with emotional arguments were shunned. There was barely even an allusion to 'selling'. It was all about *Fachwissen*. Facts are arguments:

When I want to convince someone, then I basically do so with factual arguments. (Payroll manager, German brewery)

I can only convince with facts. (Customer Services manager, German insurance company)

The German emphasis was on demonstrating the rationale behind a decision or course of action.

Both British and German managers tried to 'sell' arguments by making people think that they were their own ideas. But the British managers laid more emphasis on the need for selling. They said that persuasion was about getting others to 'buy' into your arguments. For the British middle managers, the key lay in looking at the proposition from the other person's perspective and pointing out the benefits to them: 'It's a case of thinking "what's in it for them?"' explained one of the brewing managers. It was also a question of timing, as demonstrated by the construction manager who was waiting for his boss to be in a good mood. The means of persuasion should be geared to the audience: for instance, in order to persuade a colleague to complete a process chart for his quality project in time, the quality assurance manager in the British insurance company bet him a pint of beer that he could not do it.

An interesting difference emerges between British and the German managers when it comes to persuading others: the British manager need not be *au fait* with the other person's job or duties, but with his or her psyche. This was explicitly mentioned by the production manager in the British brewery:

> I pride myself on knowing all 52 people on the shop floor, and at least five of their ten foibles. I know who supports West Ham (a football club), who does *The Times* crossword same as me, and who is as mad as a hatter. I would use that knowledge when I needed to persuade someone. You can't tell anybody to give you cooperation.'

Persuasion seemed to be built into the British model, even in relations that were ostensibly hierarchical. During the observation phase, one of the construction managers even talked about having to 'use a bit of kidology' with his secretary in order to get her to do things she did not want to do. Secretaries may be cajoled into doing work: 'Jenny, are you going to type this for us, love? Thank you, darling, you are an angel. How did the golf go yesterday?'[12]

Resorting to coercion was widely regarded as a measure of last recourse and might even be considered an admission of failure as a 'man manager'. It was tantamount to admitting that one was not up to the managerial task. One of the British brewery managers expressly made this point: 'I would never use the 'pips on the shoulder'. That's a virility test and the manager who needs that is in the wrong job.'

German managers also do not like to resort to coercion, but for different reasons: for British managers, coercion suggests a deficiency in people management; for German managers, it would imply a lack of expertise – that they did not know what they were talking about.

An integral part of the persuasion orientation of British middle managers was the routine and tactical use of humour. Humour was injected into routine requests to cancel any hint of authoritarianism. It was seen to lower resistance to decisions which were taken unilaterally or which were not easily justified. Take the example of the production manager who, needing to take the edge off an instruction, announced, 'My wife sorted out that problem last night, so this is how we are going to do it . . .'

Humour, in British organizations, is seen as the quickest way to connect with someone. It is considered not just as a valuable tool by managers, but also a valid one, in bringing people round and gaining compliance. For instance, the distribution manager in the British brewery, claimed that he would use humour when negotiations with the trade unions were getting out of hand: 'When things get heavy with the shop stewards, I'll pull this out (takes out a Groucho nose and moustache with party whistle attached) and give a blow on it.' Humour, then, underpins the persuasion mode – it helps in connecting with people, putting them into a receptive frame of mind and winning them over.

The British managers developed a wide range of contacts in order to ensure the cooperative relationships needed to enact their agendas. When asked who else (besides the compulsory contacts) they spoke to, they would typically answer, 'anybody and everybody' or 'the world and his dog'. The distribution manager in the British brewery explained that whenever he needed to contact someone he did not know – for instance at head office – he would go through someone he did know who could pave the way for him: 'You use people – even directors.'

The administration manager in the British brewery confirmed this view. He explained that he would go to whoever was most likely to give him the information he was after – 'irrespective of organizational protocol'. But this also produces an obligation to reciprocate when others want help – and this has repercussions on management work (fragmentation) and on management style (such as telephone usage). For instance, because the administration manager in the British brewery was a well-established figure with a wide range of contacts, people wanted to tap into his knowledge and at times he found it difficult to shut himself off. This led to a more fragmented work pattern than he would have liked.

Interestingly, the full extent of their networking often only became discernible on 'borderline' activities. Take the example of one of the British technical managers in the construction industry: 'I need some software.' He explained to a colleague in the purchasing department. 'Can you chase up some computers in London. Don't leave it to Ted. See what you can do. Promise him a pint, pull a few strings. We need the computers here next week.' It is in situations of no official authority, that influence, ingenuity and carefully cultivated relations come into their own.

Successful networking means extending and maintaining relationships. This requires time and interpersonal effort, as well as some natural aptitude. For instance, the brewery production manager advised a colleague about tax problems in exchange for some immediate help on the fermenting vessels; and the brewery's distribution manager nurtured relations with the security officer by letting him know that he could join them when they had their tea break in the afternoon.

In the British companies, the company structure meant that managers had contact with nearly every department as a matter of course. Some of the managers might choose to have *more* than the necessary contacts simply to make their jobs easier.

As important as the range of discretionary contacts is the *discretionary information* the British managers got out of *compulsory contacts*. The British managers seemed to devote more time than their German counterparts to picking up 'spare' information. Talking with and about others helped the British managers to predict their behaviour by providing insights into their character and motives. For the British managers it provided vital information for understanding how to persuade them or giving insight into their hidden agenda. But beyond that, such conversations are also linked with the British view of management and organizations. It reflects the British view of the organization as a village, work as a pseudo-social activity, and management as personality-driven.

Temperamentally, the British managers derived more satisfaction from social contact than the German managers seemed to do; they were comfortable in unstructured situations; their management style was more an expression of their personality.

In German companies networking does not seem to play the same essential and routine role that it does in Britain. The contacts of German middle managers are usually restricted to those with whom they have to deal for getting their jobs done. John Mole observed: 'There is not the same alliance-building across boundaries as in many companies. Informal contacts are more within functions than across boundaries.'[13]

Partly this is a result of institutional differences between the two countries: the more fragmented structure of British companies, as well as the more precarious basis of British managerial credentials, require a compensatory effort in cultivating relations.

CHECKING AND CONTROL

It was suggested at the start of this chapter that middle managers are responsible for 'keeping the show on the road'. The main feature of this function is the checking and control of their employees' work. There are many ways and means of doing this: they range from the formal (systems) to the informal (discussions); and from the concrete (work tours or checking of output) to the abstract (checking of reports or aggregate figures).

These methods of checking employee performance are used in combination, with one process often serving as a cross-check on another. The dominance of a particular type of check, however, varies considerably depending on the nature of the industry, on organizational norms and on the tasks assigned to a given department. For instance, managers in the brewing and insurance industries, in both countries, relied heavily on output-related controls such as volume of beer or numbers of outstanding claims. In the construction industry, more emphasis was placed on financial measures such as claims incurred, and profit margin.

Individual functions also have different control needs. For instance, managers in the finance-related functions, in all three industries in both countries, consistently relied on accuracy-related controls, to do with errors and deadlines. There are also organizational differences. In two of the British companies (brewing and insurance) objectives and annual reviews played a large part in the control process. Employee performance was judged on the basis of conformity to a number of quantitative and qualitative objectives at six-monthly intervals.

The industry, organizational and functional reasons for differences in formal controls used by the managers makes the British–German dimension not a useful explanatory variable. However, a cross-cultural difference was noticeable in the use of qualitative controls. This form of control is random and individually oriented, rather than systematic and department oriented. It might involve direct inspection of output, tours of the workplace, the review of special cases, conversations with the staff or feedback from others who deal with them.

The German middle managers tended to favour a specific and technical approach to checking. Typically, they would want to check the output of their subordinates personally. Similarly, they would use conversations with subordinates as a way of gauging their technical know-how. Twenty-seven of the thirty German middle managers interviewed claimed that they assessed their subordinates' expertise in this way. To do this successfully, requires the detailed knowledge of their subordinates' duties which the managers' formal qualifications and career experiences have given them.

British middle managers could only use such technical controls on a much smaller scale. Because of their career paths, and their educational background they were less likely to possess such detailed knowledge of their subordinates' duties and the relevant work processes. The managers in the British construction company were an exception to this generalization. They could judge the work of their subordinates in detail, having previously done the same work themselves:

> Through my own experience at the coal-face I can judge quickly whether someone is on the ball or not by their concerns and how alive they are to the risk that you identify. When you start talking to them, you can gauge by how quickly the problem you have identified comes into the conversation, whether it is a matter of concern or complacency, whether he has identified why it has happened, how he is going to overcome it, and how fast and at what cost. (Managing quantity surveyor, British construction company)

This statement from a manager from the British construction firm shows the same detailed understanding of the employees' work and work processes that was typical for a German middle manager:

> I can adequately determine the effectiveness of my employees only when I, personally, am familiar with the assignments given to each work-group. There are no duties, which I have not already performed myself, not only with respect to quality, but also to quantity. I know, therefore, what goes on. (Administration manager, German brewery)

The British middle managers did not, and for the reasons given may not have been able to, engage in detailed checking of their subordinates' work. They tended to check on the progress of the people rather than on the work itself. They would typically ask short, open-ended questions to find out how the section leaders were coping, to determine whether they were on top of situations (actual or prospective). One of the British insurance managers explained:

> I go a lot by how they work as a team – whether I feel we are actually achieving something, all pulling in the same direction. You can tell from the morale of teams whether the section leaders are doing their job properly.

This view was endorsed by one of the British construction managers:

> The easy route is always, 'How much profit did you make?' and I think it is totally the wrong route. The best way is by personal

contact. It has to be a matter of judgement and I don't know how you put it on paper.

From the observation phase, it was noticeable that the British managers were continually asking questions. Mostly these were very open-ended: 'How is the section?', 'Any problems?', 'Anything I need to know about?'. The intention was not to catch subordinates out on specific tasks, but to gain an impression of the confidence they could have in them, their ability to cope with their workload and their capacity for extra responsibility.

When the British managers did check the work itself, they were more concerned with overall feel than with technicalities. Their assessment was more likely to be based on a tour of the workplace, than on any given piece of work. As one of the British construction managers explained:

The most important thing is the feel of the job when you walk around it – is there a lot of industry, can you see that things are being done properly? You might have lots of bits of paper that tell you it is being done properly, but if materials are not being stored properly, if things are not being done in the proper sequence, if a reasonable level of protection is not in place, then all the bits of paper in the world won't convince me that the job is being run properly.

The distribution manager in the British brewery also relied heavily on observation to assess the effectiveness of his staff:

I use my own eyes and ears. I can see whether they're working, whether they're skiving, whether they're doing what's expected of them.

This emphasis on checking by observation was especially noticeable during the site visits conducted by the British construction managers. These visits enabled them to check on how things were being done, the accuracy of reports they had been receiving, the morale of the site team, and the capabilities and expectations of subordinates. Visits were systematically rounded off with a general query like, 'Anything else of any concern at all?'

For the British managers, intervention in the actual work of their subordinates was exceptional. Indeed, technical problems coming up from below were likely to be interpreted quite differently from the way they would be interpreted in Germany. The German managers expected problems from below. However much they may have claimed the contrary, British managers did not, as a rule, expect to have to deal with technical problems. One often heard the comment, in Britain, that 'My boss judges my effectiveness by the number of problems that come through to him.' Thus, problems coming through to the middle managers were likely to cause a revision of their subordinates' competence. As one of the construction managers put it:

> It's only if there are problems and wheels start dropping off all over the place that you have to start thinking, have I got the right people in the right jobs, or are they being trained properly?

The British managers were not there primarily to deal with the technical problems which arose so much as the human problems of teamwork, motivation, development and so on. That is what they checked on and what they were most comfortable solving.

UNDERSTANDING OF MANAGEMENT

The German middle manager's understanding of management was mainly characterized by a technical orientation. This could, to a large extent, be traced back to a direct relationship between the professional training of the manager and the department for which he or she was responsible, and to the narrow functional career path which was typical for German managers.

The strong technical orientation of the German middle managers manifested itself in the responsibilities that they chose to emphasize. An attempt to categorize the middle managers' questionnaire answers gave the following results. Twenty of the German middle managers surveyed mentioned specific aspects of their technical tasks, and some of them gave detailed descriptions of the manner in which these tasks were carried out. Eight of the German middle managers gave rather general descriptions of their job responsibilities. Their answers were often in the form of a repetition of their job title. 'I am the sales director for the sales territory. I am responsible for beverage wholesaling and for gastronomy' (Sales Manager, German brewery). Only two middle managers did not relate their answers at all to their technical responsibilities.

The German managers' identification with managerial responsibilities was much less than that of the British. Half the German middle managers surveyed did not even mention managerial responsibilties, while eleven managers referred to them in general, for example, 'the supervision of the department, that the work process functions well . . .' (Customer Service Manager, German insurance). Only four of the middle managers mentioned specific aspects of their managerial responsibilities.

The British middle managers considered their main responsibilities to be more the managerial tasks of their position. They emphasized technical responsibilities less often than the German middle managers. Tables 5.6 and 5.7 present an overview of the different orientations of German and British middle managers from their answers to the interview questionnaire.

What is striking from a comparison of Tables 5.6 and 5.7 is that the British and German managers differed in whether they gave technical or managerial descriptions of their responsibilities and in whether they went into detail about them. The British managers tended not to

Table 5.6   Identification of technical responsibilities

Identification of job-related (technical) responsibilities	German middle managers	British middle managers
No identification	2	11
General identification	8	18
Identific./description of specific aspects	20	1

Table 5.7   Identification of managerial responsibilities

Identification of managerial responsibilities	German middle managers	British middle managers
No identification	15	6
General identification	11	18
Identification/description of specific aspects	4	6

go into much detail on either, but simply to elaborate on the job title. They viewed themselves as generalists. This difference in German and British middle managers' understanding of management became even more clear in the aspects of their tasks that they considered to be most important. Here, the British middle managers gave first priority to managerial tasks in which a large number emphasize the activities of people management.

The general idea was that making people feel part of the team was the precursor to getting the best out of them. For the British middle managers, the technical aspects of their jobs were secondary.

> Planning and production are easy – it is getting the people to work wholeheartedly that is the challenge. (Brewing and fermenting manager, British brewery)

> I would say a good working relationship with my peers and the people directly under my control is the most important responsibility. (Regional buyer, British construction company)

> It is important for me to make sure that everybody is working in a happy environment. If people are unhappy, they are not going to work at their most efficient. (Estimating manager, British construction company)

> Ensuring that the staff are settled and well communicated with. (Regional administrator, British construction company)

> Development of the people that work for me – their personal satisfaction of doing the job. (Renewals manager, British insurance company)

> The management of the staff. I see a need to create a team environment and I spend a lot of time developing the team identity within my own management team. (Existing business manager, British insurance company)

The emphasis on strictly managerial responsibilities, as opposed to technical responsibilities, contrasted with the answers given by the German managers. Although people management was an important aspect of German middle managers' responsibilities, it was not so central. The task was seen more as achieving a smooth allocation of work duties within the department and maintaining a positive work climate. The difference between German and British managers was in this respect one of emphasis. This became clear in the responses of the German middle managers. Only five spontaneously cited managerial tasks as the most important aspect of their job. Ten German managers began by speaking about their job-related duties and only mentioned managerial tasks when prompted. The German answers demonstrate a perceived oneness, or inseparability, of technical duties and managerial responsibilities:

> Actually, the most important aspect would be managerial responsibility. But when I do not participate in any job-related tasks, I lose the overview. And, therefore, I perform technical duties so that I do not lose the overview concerning my managerial responsibilities. (Commercial branch manager, German construction company)

Technical duties could take a large portion of a German middle manager's day. On the contrary, middle managers in Britain preferred a 'hands-off' approach. Although they saw themselves as being responsible for fulfilling the duties of their department, they did not want to become personally involved. They saw their duty much more as getting their subordinates to accomplish the tasks necessary for achieving departmental goals. They seemed keen to distance themselves from technical involvement.

The British managers were very conscious of the split between managerial work and technical work. These were not seen as two sides of the same coin. Rather, they represented a hierarchical threshold. In Britain, technical work was seen as something to be abandoned in the search for promotion into management.[14]

Management through 'expert knowledge' (Management by *Fachwissen*) seems to be the dominant way in which German middle managers understood management.[15] Middle managers in Germany had a technical understanding of management which did not reflect the role of the manager as described in the management literature. They would talk of their jobs and their work, but the British middle managers in contrast spontaneously talked in terms of their role as a manager.

The German managers were not so well-versed in the vernacular of management. Many had clearly not been exposed to management as a discipline. Their answers were clichéd, they found it hard to distance themselves from their jobs, or to imagine what other managers could possibly learn from knowing how they did their particular jobs.

Technical expertise was important to the German middle managers in our study for another reason. It was the means by which they legitimatized their authority. This 'culture of mastery' extended all the way to the top. According to Eberwein and Tholen,[16] German senior managers also relied on technical expertise as the basis of their authority.

The supervisory role was rejected by almost every one of the German middle managers who were interviewed. Only five of them used 'boss' or 'superior' to describe their formal position in the organizational hierarchy. Three of the five, along with one other middle manager, used the analogy of supervisor-team-leader to bring themselves closer to the level of their subordinates. Seventeen of the thirty middle managers explicitly rejected the role of superior, for example:

I want to be viewed as a normal employee, not as a superior. (Accounting manager, German insurance company)

I do not want to be seen as a strict superior, more as a colleague. (Commercial branch manager, German construction company).

Yes, it is actually more important to me to be viewed as a colleague who supervises, but not necessarily as a superior. (Maintenance manager, German brewery)

This rejection of the role of superior may reflect two things: first, the identification downwards, rather than upwards, because of the restrictions on German managers and the difficulty of breaking into the upper ranks, for want of academic credentials; second, it shows a certain self-confidence, based on technical probity – the German managers did not have to distance themselves artificially from their subordinates to be respected. They earned their respect simply by being better at their jobs than their subordinates. The German emphasis was on being *an* authority rather than being *in* authority.

German middle managers not only perceived themselves as colleagues who supervise, they saw it as very important for them to set a 'good example' and to provide a 'role model' for their staff. In accordance with this belief, they often forwent managerial privileges:

I still clock in as an example to the others . . . I do not want to be privileged because I am the head of the department. I would like to say that I have the same rights and duties as every employee. (Commercial branch manager, German construction company)

If we consider how German managers wanted to be seen by their subordinates, it becomes clear that they relied heavily on their technical expertise as a basis for their authority:

I would like to be seen as a person who is worthy and competent enough to fulfil my position 100 per cent. (Administration manager, German brewery)

That I perform my functional tasks. That when a subordinate has a question, he can turn to me. (Claims processing manager, German insurance company)

I would like to be viewed as an employee who is able to do anything, who can take corrective action when something goes wrong. (Commercial branch manager, German construction company)

At the same time, these answers seem to underline Handy's observation about business executives' understanding of management in Germany . . . 'management, as a concept of its own, divorced from what is to be managed, is not widely understood or accepted'.[17] This was also evident from the responses to our open-ended request for guidelines to successful management. Thirteen of the thirty German middle managers interviewed were puzzled by the question and either answered with general statements or tended to repeat prior answers (referring to the necessary technical expertise or rejecting their role as a superior). Only six managers named factors which were important to them and which actually corresponded to images of managers and their tasks presented in the management literature:

- to set goals and to guide employees in meeting these goals (four middle managers);
- to use subordinates according to their qualifications and to motivate them (two middle managers).

It is interesting to note that four middle managers explicitly referred to structure (of the company or of the department) as a key to successful management:

The most important influencing factor is the structure of the company. It has to be right. Without that, you cannot work well or effectively. It is structure that determines responsibility. (Commercial branch manager, German construction company)

The equivalent response in Britain was to state that the aim was to play to people's strengths and to build teams, which complemented each other. British middle managers were mostly of the opinion that a department should be built around individual strength rather than insisting on filling prearranged slots. This answer was much more people-focused than structure-oriented. The onus was on the creative input of the individual manager, on his or her ability to put together a team. In Germany, the emphasis was on getting the structure right to start with, then filling the jobs with the right people. The task was seen as fitting people to jobs rather than fitting jobs to people.

The British middle managers were more likely to see themselves as scaled-down senior managers, to talk of developing their subordinates and giving them the means and motivation to do a good job – such answers indicated that the British middle managers, implicitly at least, thought of themselves as bosses.

I want to give the people the means of doing their job to the best of their ability. (Packaging manager, British brewery)

The most important thing is to keep my staff happy and motivated – because if they are not, you will not get a good day's work out of them. (Administration manager, British brewery)

The British middle managers' answers to the question of personal guidelines for successful management were also far richer and lengthier. They seemed prepared to philosophize spontaneously about management. The dominant themes were fairness, listening, communication, honesty, integrity and an ability to understand people, how they think, and to put oneself in their position. All this reflected a greater managerial consciousness in British companies:

Management is really about understanding human nature and adjusting your style to suit. If you give people a full appreciation of why they are doing something, make them feel part of a team, then you get a better response from them. (Administration manager, British brewery)

The crux is for the people under and over you to know that they can trust your judgement. (Shift manager, British brewery)

Never underestimate the importance of people. You have to try to coax and develop them to the best of their potential, because that will help you. (Existing business manager, British insurance)

I do not have a slogan, but I think you have to give people freedom to manoeuvre, and recognition. (Sales manager, British insurance)

Successful management can only be based on good communication. I think there is nothing worse than managers talking to other managers but not talking to their staff and involving them. (Managing quantity surveyor, British construction)

It all comes down to people. If you cannot get on with people, if you cannot motivate people, then you should not be in the job. (Administration manager, British construction company)

The British managers were full of folk wisdom and insights gleaned from their experience in *dealing with people*. There was never any hint, in their answers, that management was challenging in a technical sense. All their answers revolved around relationships, social skills and the way the manager was perceived. They understood themselves to be people-managers and they saw their ability as people-managers to be the key to advancing to a higher managerial position. Managerial status in this group of British middle managers was presented as deriving from skill in handling people, not so much from expertise or demonstrable professionalism.

The managers observed in Britain clearly viewed their roles differently from the German managers and this difference was evident in their behaviour. They emphasized their supervisory role by setting their own work-schedule and break-periods, by organizing their departments and introducing new task areas. They saw it as their role to take 'the larger view' and to ensure that subordinates were doing properly what had been delegated to them. One possible explanation for the different behaviour of German and British middle managers may have lain in the fact that British executives in general did not draw their authority from their technical qualifications and this made it necessary to establish their managerial position in other ways. Because of their lack of direct contact with the work, British managers were highly exposed and therefore relied on the loyalty, integrity and honesty of their subordinates. This may also help to explain their emphasis on people-management and team-building.

Part III

Explaining the Differences

6 Management and Organizational Structure

THE INFLUENCE OF ORGANIZATIONAL STRUCTURE, CONTEXT, AND CULTURE ON THE ROLES AND BEHAVIOUR OF MIDDLE MANAGERS

The Causal Scheme

The roles and behaviours of the middle managers studied in Britain and Germany differed considerably, as shown in the previous chapters. To recapitulate on a few of these differences:

- Formal qualifications are more important for a career in middle management in Germany than in Britain.
- German middle managers exhibit a more technical orientation towards their jobs while their British colleagues stress the general management tasks of their jobs.
- Communication of German middle managers with their subordinates is predominantly task-oriented while that of their British counterparts concentrates on motivation, reaching agreement on targets, and getting general policies implemented.
- German middle managers spend significantly more time alone than British ones.
- For British middle managers meetings are the preferred method for achieving coordination, while German middle managers rely very much on establishing routines or programs. Consequently, British middle managers spend considerably more time in scheduled and unscheduled meetings than their German colleagues.
- German middle managers make more telephone calls than the British ones but the average length of their phone calls is shorter.
- German middle managers have more ad hoc contacts but, again, the average duration of their face-to-face contacts is shorter.
- In order to enlist support British middle managers rely first of all on persuasion and networking. Their German colleagues trust that they can convince others, primarily by the content of their arguments, not the presentation.

131

● German middle managers apply predominantly process control in order to check the work of their subordinates, while their British colleagues prefer output (progress) control.

How can these differences between roles and behaviour of British and German middle managers be explained? We think that three sets of factors have to be taken into account:

1. organizational structure;
2. context factors such as technology, size of organization or complexity and dynamics of the environment;
3. cultural factors such as value systems or societal institutions such as qualification systems or patterns of industrial relations.

These sets of factors are highly interdependent: context factors like technology influence roles and behaviour directly and indirectly through organizational structure. Cultural factors also affect roles and behaviour directly and indirectly by shaping context factors and organizational structures which are embedded in culture. This leads us to the causal scheme shown in Figure 6.1.

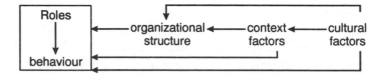

Figure 6.1   Factors influencing managerial roles and behaviour

This chapter will concentrate on the influences of organizational structure and context on managerial roles and behaviour. We will also discuss those influences of culture which are mediated by organizational structure. The more direct influences of culture are dealt with in Chapters 7 and 8 which analyse how institutions, such as the qualification and value systems of the two cultures impinge on managerial roles and behaviour.

Managerial Roles and Behaviour: Given or Negotiated?

Does organizational structure determine the behaviour of organizational members? Max Weber was convinced that it does. For him the restrictions inherent in formal structure were so strong that bureaucracies were equated with 'iron cages' leaving no room for self-responsible actions.[1] The proponents of the contingency approach, who see themselves in the tradition of Weber, also stress the constraints imposed by formal organizational structure on the roles and behaviour of organizations' members.[2] They argue that it is through the formal structure that tasks are assigned to departments and individual jobs. The organizational structure also influences roles and behaviour by demarcating decision competences and by defining relationships of super- and subordination and spans of control. By providing programmes, planning procedures, team structures and hierarchies, it also determines which mode of coordination prevails for specific tasks.[3]

Interactionist role theory assumes a contrasting position. Proponents of this theory argue that the roles of organization members are not simply given by pre-existing formal rules and learned passively, but that the roles are the product of ongoing negotiating processes.[4] According to this theory, roles are created through repeated interactions in which common understandings emerge about which activities are relevant, which goals should be pursued, and how the internal and external environment should be interpreted.[5] In this perspective, formal structure is more an outcome than a precondition of coordinated activities in organizations: organization members agree on certain rules or they agree to interpret existing rules in a specific way.

Some convergence between the two positions can be observed.[6] The 'structuralists' concede that role expectations, even in organizations, are often highly contradictory and incomplete so that negotiation on roles in ongoing interactions is unavoidable. The 'interactionists', on the other hand, admit that in some situations, especially in formal organizations, severe limitations are imposed on the process of role-making.[7]

Our own approach is interactionistic in so far as we assume that the interactions of middle managers with members of their role-set lead to more or less conformity between the role expectations expressed by superiors and the role interpretations of middle managers. However, we also assume that formal organizational structures considerably constrain the role interpretations which are acceptable for particular jobs.

Anglo-German Organizational Differences: Findings of Other Research

A summary of earlier research can show whether the differences in organizational structures which we found in comparing our British and German companies are similar to those reported in other studies. If they are, this would show that the differences have survived the major restructuring that has taken place, especially in large British companies, since the date of these studies. There are no comparable recent studies.

In the late 1970s – the date of the main studies – German companies were found, on average, to have wider spans of control at almost every level, but especially at the supervisory level, than British companies and, consequently, flatter hierarchies.[8] The proportion of staff employees within the total workforce was also lower in German companies. While British companies tended to create extra jobs for specialized knowledge at all levels from the shop-floor upwards, German companies tended to incorporate specialist and technical expertise in the line itself.[9] This caused organizations to grow more laterally in Britain, thus requiring more extensive lateral contacts.

The degree of formalization was also found to be higher in British companies than in German ones in so far as the use of job descriptions, organization charts and other written procedures was concerned.[10] This was attributed by Lane to the flatter organizational structure in Germany which allows coordination by less formal means.[11] The degree of formalization, however, should not be confused with the extent of rule-oriented behaviour. Some authors hold that the Germans do not have to have rules in written form since they know them by heart and that for the British written procedures are evidence of a losing battle against rule deviating behaviour in management.[12]

Control seemed to be more highly centralized in German business organizations.[13] This could be, at least partly, attributed to flatter organizational structures in German companies which allowed for effective operation of centralized control.

In a study made in the late 1970s Horovitz found strategic planning to be more developed in Britain than in Germany where long-range planning covered fewer years,[14] was less formalized, and involved a smaller number of people. On the other hand, Budde *et al.* pointed out a 'greater tendency for West German management to adopt a proactive and long-term view of business opportunity'.[15] Lawrence also generally found forward planning more developed in Germany with a superior capacity for anticipating difficulties and for preparing contingency plans.[16] Lane speculated

that the formal properties of the British planning system identified by Horovitz remain ineffective because they address themselves insufficiently to the relevant issues – they remain too narrowly focused on finance and thus do not generate clear objectives to be pursued by management at the lower levels.[17]

With respect to short-term planning, Horovitz reported higher degrees of participation in the one-year planning cycle in Germany.[18]

Horovitz identified a preference in British companies for a style of control which provides loose guidance rather than viewing control as an instrument for correcting deviances from plans.[19] He found a higher degree of consistency between detailed planning data and the mode in which control was exercised in German companies. He concluded that 'in Germany, the control systems appear to be much more stringent and oriented towards corrective action than in France or Great Britain.'

Horovitz also found that control information in Britain was often qualitative in nature, oriented towards future performance, and heavily biased toward financial control. In German companies, control information was prepared by central staffs; it was mostly in qualitative form and tended to be operations-oriented.[20]

ANGLO-GERMAN ORGANIZATIONAL DIFFERENCES: IMPACT ON ROLES AND BEHAVIOUR

Since organizational structures are embedded in the culture and, more specifically, are part of industry structures which have evolved historically in unique ways in each country, it is impossible to find two organizations in different cultures which are perfectly matched. For our study this meant taking into account differences in organizational structures between our matched cases which might influence the roles and behaviours of middle managers. In other words: managers in the two cultures may behave differently not only because their attitudes are moulded by the societal context, but also because they work in different organizational settings which constrain their behaviour in specific ways. Differences in structures between organizations of different cultures can either be 'culturally neutral' – perhaps caused by differences in sizes of organization or in production programmes – or they can reflect recurrent cultural preferences in structural design, such as a greater tendency towards centralization of decision-making or formalization in one culture. Thus, on closer inspection one often finds that many of these 'culturally neutral' differences are actually conditioned by culture.

For instance, differences in the size of companies might be caused by different industry traditions or by more or less rigorous anti-trust legislation, and differences in production programmes might stem from deep-seated cultural differences in consumer tastes.

It is, therefore, important to determine in what ways and to what extent the differences in roles and behaviours of British and German managers, reported in the previous chapters, are attributable to differences in organizational structure. Perhaps the middle managers in the two cultures are not so different after all, but it is the organizational structures, in which they work, and which force them to define their roles and to behave in different ways.

In the following section we shall summarize the main similarities and differences between the British and the German organizations in each of the three industries (a detailed description of the organizational differences can be found in Chapter 2). We shall also consider to what extent these differences fit the general patterns found in previous Anglo-German comparisons of organizations. In the final section we shall discuss how differences between our British and German organizations and their contexts could have influenced the roles and behaviours of the middle managers studied.

Breweries

The British and German breweries were, as shown in more detail in Chapter 2, of comparable size. The organizational structures were also very similar in their functional grouping.

The core technology in both breweries could be characterized as process technology in Woodward's terms.[21] In an automated way ingredients were put together to brew a certain volume of beer which, after being stored for some time in tanks, was packaged into containers of different sorts, either kegs or bottles. The packaging process was also performed as a highly automated operation.

Coordination between sales and production in the British brewery was accomplished with the support of a computer system which picked up the orders from depots, took account of the previous year and projected forward so that the brewery could plan the purchase of raw materials, as well as the brewing and packaging processes over a four week brewing cycle. During the course of the four-weeks, the depots refined the accuracy of the information. For example, if the original forecast was 1000 barrels; the following week it might be changed to 1100; in two weeks to 1080; and when it came to the actual order it might be 1085. The communication chain ran from sales accounts to depots, to the breweries. Within the brewery, the information went to the operations manager in the technical department who planned the brewing schedule for the production department.

In the German brewery, there was also a long-term production plan. However, demand was more susceptible to short-term fluctuations primarily because the distribution channels of the German brewery differed considerably. The selling of beer through 'tied' outlets took only a part of the turnover. Most of the beer is sold by trade companies. As a result the actual production plan was agreed upon in a weekly meeting between sales and production for the following week.

The middle managers of the British and German breweries faced different degrees of complexity in their roles because of many differences in the markets they served. The German brewery was producing and selling more varieties of beer, with more varied packaging, through more distribution channels within Germany and abroad than the British company. It had its own sales department, and its middle managers were involved in coordinating the activities of subsidiaries. Complexity was further increased during the period of our study because of the reunification of Germany which meant tough competition for market shares in new markets. It was only in industrial relations that the managers of the German brewery were faced with less complexity than their British colleagues: union membership was low in the German brewery and disputes with the works councils were usually handled by the personnel managers.

Empirical research has shown that the complexity and dynamics of the environment are positively correlated with greater formalization,[22] decentralization, and a higher incidence of scheduled and unscheduled meetings.[23]

A comparison of the formalization in the two breweries did not corroborate these findings: the British brewery seemed to be characterized by a higher degree of formalization. However, this finding was in line with results of Anglo-German comparisons of organizations. These revealed a general tendency towards greater formalization among British companies. Also the greater weight placed on financial control as opposed to operational control in the British brewery corresponded to previous Anglo-German comparisons.

We can hypothesize that because of greater environmental complexity and dynamics, coordination needs should be higher for the German middle managers.

The packaging managers in the two breweries have the most similar roles, amongst the managers we studied. So they can best be used to compare how similar they really are and how and why their types of activities and contacts vary. The packaging managers in both breweries were responsible for the planning and operation of the packaging process. In both packaging departments the process was automated in the same way: the beer produced and stored in tanks waiting to be packaged was filled automatically into kegs or bottles. These were prepared automatically for the process, that is, washed, controlled and transported to the proper place where they were packaged.

While this process was technologically fairly simple its complexity varied with the containers to be processed. In the British brewery these were kegs which usually did not vary in size or shape. The sort of beer produced and packaged on any one line did not vary either. In the German brewery the packaging was much more complex. Not only were there at least three sorts of beer to be packaged on any one line but also the size and shape of bottles varied according to the intended market. Similarly different national markets required different labels. The packaging material, glass, contributed to the complexity of the process because of its fragility.

Despite the similarities in the technology, the two packaging managers had somewhat different tasks. Their planning role differed because the planning process was more complex and time-consuming in the German brewery because of the variety of products and bottles to be packaged. In the British brewery the process was planned more continuously and predictably despite problems in selling. While the German packaging manager had to react frequently to sudden changes in demands from the sales force, the British packaging manager had not.

The tasks of the two managers also differed in checking and control. There was little need for the British packaging manager to control the process once it had started unless there were major problems with the machinery. The German packaging manager had to intervene more often in order to control the process because of the uncertainties described above. He had constantly to be ready to control machinery and materials, for example, the supply of empty bottles appropriate for the kind of beer to be packaged and the country of destination. This, in his eyes, was a fairly complex task: 'it is important to package large quantities [for economic reasons because of the long supply time of the machinery, our addition] and to coordinate with the sales department.' 'You have ten to twelve different orders for one week . . . you have to be careful to order the amount [of empty bottles] you need – this has to be performed that very week, otherwise it accumulates and you will not make it' (Packaging Manager, German brewery).

The packaging managers in both countries have to check the output of their department, but the complexity of the process in the German brewery meant that the German packaging manager had to make more varied checks than his British counterpart. The British packaging manager checked the output using his VDU which constantly provided him with all the relevant data. He could easily check the results against the planned quantity and hence react immediately should there be any discrepancies. The German packaging manager usually checked the reports of each of his packaging plants only once a day. In order to do so he checked the display in the control room, where the output of any one line was displayed on a continuous basis. The most important item for him was the degree of efficiency since it gave indications of difficulties which he should tackle. Thus, the daily report of his plants was the starting-point for further checks, technical or organizational, if there were problems with efficiency. The kind of checking and the complexity of the process therefore stemmed from the different work situations of the packaging managers, these being dependent on the technology applied.

The number of breakdowns caused by the higher complexity of the process in the German brewery meant that greater cooperation was needed with other departments such as sales, distribution, and maintenance in order to coordinate resultant changes to previous planning. Cooperation with other departments for the British packaging manager was far less affected by technological problems, since the packaging department was much more buffered against uncertainties from the environment, hence technology could be applied more smoothly.

The data reflected this higher complexity of the packaging job in the German brewery (Tables 6.1 and 6.2). The German packaging manager attended more scheduled meetings and he spent a larger part of his working day in these meetings. He also had almost twice as many fleeting contacts as did his British counterpart. However, these contacts altogether took relatively less of his working time. He had three times as many communication episodes with his subordinates, though these episodes altogether used up only slightly more of his working time in comparison to the time his counterpart communicated with subordinates.

Table 6.1 Activities of German and British packaging managers over total observation (each was observed for three days)

| Type of activity | Packaging Manager | | | |
| | German | | British | |
	av. no./day	% of working time	av. no./day	% of working time
Desk work	48	28.7	21	25.8
Telephone	22	8.3	26	12.8
Scheduled meetings	2	11.5	1	6.3
Unscheduled meetings	2	12.7	1	7.6
Further contacts	97	38.8	30	45.2
Other			2	2.3

Table 6.2 Communication episodes of German and British packaging managers over total observation

| Communication episodes | German | | British | |
	av. no./day	% of working time	av. no./day	% of working time
With bosses			1	1.2
With peers	23	11.5	25	27.6
With subs	93	35.6	26	25.4
With outsiders	4	3.6	1	2.2
Mixed	3	20.6	5	15.5

There seems to be no reason to think that these days were atypical. The observation data on packaging managers deviate from the general picture found in our research insofar as the German manager has more scheduled and unscheduled meetings. However, given the differences in complexity and dynamics of the environment, it is surprising that the difference in the incidence of meetings is not more marked.

The distribution managers constituted another pair of jobs which seemed highly comparable. (The observation data are given in Tables 6.3 and 6.4.) The German distribution manager had fewer unscheduled meetings than his British colleague despite the greater complexity of the German manager's coordination task (neither manager had any scheduled meetings during the observation). Only his higher number of fleeting contacts seems to reflect the higher degree of complexity in his job. He had more communication episodes with peers, subordinates and outsiders but these took less time than his British counterpart.

Table 6.3 Activities of German and British distribution managers over total observation (each was observed for two days)

| Type of activity | Distribution Manager | | | |
| | German | | British | |
	av. no./day	% of working time	av. no./day	% of working time
Desk work	45	37.6	13	7.8
Telephone	38	21.7	30	17.3
Scheduled meetings				
Unscheduled meetings	1	2.5	2	27.5
Further contacts	82	38.2	50	43.1
Other			3	4.3

Table 6.4 Communication episodes of German and British distribution managers over total observation

Communication episodes	German		British	
	av. no./day	% of working time	av. no./day	% of working time
With bosses	1	2.1	2	1.1
With peers	29	19.4	16	25.0
With subs	80	35.9	57	48.3
With outsiders	11	5.0	6	5.5
Mixed			1	8.0

Thus, the influence of the organizational structures is visible in these data, but the general differences between British and German managers which were established in the previous chapters are also strongly reflected.

The comparisons of the two pairs of managers show that even when the most comparable jobs are selected there are still considerable differences in their organizational setting. However, the general differences between British and German managers discussed in the previous chapters are illustrated by these examples.

Life Assurances

The main differences in the organization structures and environments of the British and German insurance companies were described in Chapter 2: if life assurance contracts only are taken into account, the German company was somewhat larger than the British one. The British company operated in a more complex and dynamic environment: the British insurance market was less regulated than the German one which led to more types of life assurance policies in Britain. Deregulation in Britain has encouraged banks and building societies to diversify into life assurances. Overall, competition is greater in Britain.

The degree of formalization in the British company appeared to be higher than in the German one. This contradicts findings quoted earlier on the relationship between organizational size and formalization, but is in line with findings on the influence of environmental complexity and dynamics on formalization as well as with results from British–German comparisons of organizations.

Looking at technology, significant differences between the British and the German company could be identified: computer-based support in the German company was more advanced than in the British one. The computer system in Germany was of the type *'integrierte Sachbearbeitung'* (integrated processing of cases). This meant each clerk in the customer services department could perform all operations by using a word-processor with text modules, in a paperless fashion, for nearly all types of policies which can possibly occur in dealing with customers: he or she could put in new contracts, alter existing ones, pay out claims, handle surrenders and answer customers' questions. In the British company some functions got some support from the computer system, but not in such an integrated fashion.

The automation and integration of operations in the German life assurance company was facilitated by the high degree of regulation in the life assurance market in Germany which had led to a high degree of standardization of contracts. This, in turn, had enabled the German company to implement a radical structural change: grouping by customers instead of by functions. This change has considerably increased departmental autonomy. A clerk in a customer service subdepartment never has to turn to other departments in order to get information to solve a problem in dealing with a customer. It is interesting that a quality control department did not exist in the German company. Even before the major restructuring it did not exist.

If a highly automated and integrated clerical information technology is implemented, it is not too difficult to extend its support to tasks of middle management. This had happened in the German insurance company: most of the tasks of the middle managers, such as coordinating the work process in the department, allocating tasks to workers, checking the labour process, etc., were facilitated by computer programmes.

The autonomy of clerks and departments in the German insurance company considerably reduced the coordination tasks of middle managers, at least in the customer services departments. One remaining task, which was legally restricted to them, was to release damage claims that exceeded a certain amount of money, but even this task was much facilitated by technology. All the manager had to do was to look into the case on the VDU, check the operations performed by his or her subordinate and release the sum automatically. There was one exception to computer-aided work: in difficult cases the manager had to see the original file. His/her qualifications and experience were required to handle the case, since this minority of difficult cases had not yet been standardized. Such cases were also one of the reasons why the middle managers had to coordinate with their peers from other departments in order to agree on a common procedure. There were plans to standardize even these difficult cases so that the coordination tasks and interventions by middle managers will probably reduce even more.

The main task of the managers in the German life assurance company was to check through the information system. Unlike their British counterparts they had almost no managerial tasks apart from the responsibility for their subordinates' motivation and human relations. Even the need to coordinate with peers was much reduced by information technology, since each department was highly autonomous.

In comparison with the British company, coordination needs were also considerably reduced by an environment which was less complex and dynamic than the British one. Therefore, we could expect that middle managers in the German insurance company would have less communication with peers and subordinates than their British colleagues. Since this difference has already been established as a general pattern, which distinguished our samples of British and German managers, we expected that the differences in communication patterns between managers of the two cultures would be greater for the managers in life assurance companies than for those in the other companies. The data in Tables 6.5 and 6.6 provide some check on this expectation.

In Tables 6.5 and 6.6 the patterns of activities and communication for the three British and the four German insurance managers who work in customer service departments are compared. The differences in activity patterns are clearly in the expected direction. The British insurance managers spent 34 per cent of their working time in scheduled and unscheduled meetings as compared with only 2 per cent for the German managers. This difference was stronger than for the total sample (see Table 5.6, Chapter 5). However, the data on communication episodes is more mixed: coordination with peers took up about twice as much of the working time of British managers;

Table 6.5   Activities of German and British insurance managers in
customer service departments over the total observation

| Type of activity | Managers in customer service departments | | | |
| | German | | British | |
	av. no./day	% of working time	av. no./day	% of working time
Desk work	61	60.9	33	35.5
Telephone	24	12.4	14	5.6
Scheduled meetings			1	16.0
Unscheduled meetings	1	2.1	2	18.1
Further contacts	61	22.7	18	18.5
Other	1	1.9	3	6.3

Table 6.6   Communication episodes of German and British insurance
managers in customer service departments over total
observation

| Communication episodes | German | | British | |
	av. no./day	% of working time	av. no./day	% of working time
With bosses	4	1.7	1	0.7
With peers	8	4.7	11	10.9
With subs	62	22.2	20	31.9
With outsiders	11	6.9	2	3.8
Mixed	1	1.7	1	10.9

however, communication with subordinates was more frequent for the German managers. The subordinates still had to clear difficult cases with their bosses. The complexity of their tasks had been increased since each employee had to deal with all types of assurances. Each of the four German managers and the three British managers were observed for two days.

Construction Companies

As we have shown in Chapter 2, the German construction company was similar to the British one insofar as both had highly autonomous regions. However, there was one major difference: the British company was first organized according to divisions and then the divisions had their regional organizations, while in the German company the regional organization structure came first and was then divided into divisions.

The construction industry's technology was one-off production. Customers, such as architects, project development companies or public bodies 'ordered' projects from the construction companies, who were then responsible for the implementation of the projects, albeit in close contact with the customer so that frequent changes occurred and had to be taken into account during the construction process. This creates a quite different work situation for the managers in this industry compared with those in the two other industries studied. The production process was much more dynamic and uncertain than in the other two industries. The market was also more difficult because substantial information had to be obtained about each project, and this could be difficult.

The middle managers' tasks of controlling and checking in the construction industry were quite different from those in the production departments of the brewing or insurance companies. For them control started at the very beginning of a company/customer relationship because their early participation in the design of the product was required by the technology. Unlike the other two industries there was no standardized product but each was an individual product and there could be wide variations between products. For the control of the labour process this meant a constant cooperation and coordination with the junior managers on the sites. But it also meant seeking the customers' agreement for the stages of the labour process.

To reduce the uncertainties of one-off production, there was in the German construction company a standardized checking procedure, using information technology programmes, which was crucial, particularly for checking by the commercial managers. There was an elaborate system of calculating plans and results in terms of costs, turnover objectives and deadlines which was used to check customers' payments on contractual deadlines. If a customer failed to meet the payment deadlines this was a signal for the managers to look into the project more closely. The system enabled managers to keep abreast of problems at a particular site and thus to be able to intervene in good time.

A one-off type of production required considerable cooperation between managers. The commercial managers supplied the technical managers with the aggregated data they needed to perform their managerial tasks, such as control of the projects. The service departments, such as planning, estimation and machinery, at the region supplied project managers with resources that were too scarce and expensive to be located at each project.

In the German company, an information system provided data on project plans and ongoing costs, invoices issued and payments received. So the commercial managers could check whether a project developed according to the plan. The technical managers also used this system, since deviations in costs or payments could signal technical problems. Because of the high degree of computerization, the head office of the German company was always well-informed on the profit situation of the local companies.

In the British company, there was a monthly review of current contracts. The figures were prepared by the site quantity surveyor and showed the anticipated profit. This was a subjective assessment and the job of the managing quantity surveyor, when reporting upwards, was to indicate whether the assessment was pessimistic or optimistic.

The cost and value of construction projects was monitored weekly, monthly and quarterly, by the project manager and his superiors. Information technology was less developed than in the German company. IT did not impinge on the work of the British middle managers observed.

How would one expect the contextual factors and the organizational structure to influence roles and behaviours of middle managers in the British and German construction companies? Overall, one expected that a technology of unit production and a highly complex and dynamic environment, would mean that the middle managers would spend more time communicating, both in total time and in the frequency of brief contacts than in the other industries studied. However, the organization of the German construction company, with its integration of technical and commercial project management should reduce the need for face-to-face coordination.

In Tables 6.7 and 6.8 the activity and communication patterns of the most similar jobs in the two companies, the German project manager and the British contracts manager, are compared.

Table 6.7   Activities of German and British site managers over total observation (each was observed for two days)

| Type of activity | Site managers | | | |
| | German | | British | |
	av. no./day	% of working time	av. no./day	% of working time
Desk work	15	17.3	29	22.7
Telephone	11	8.0	10	5.4
Scheduled meetings	1	17.4	1	6.4
Unscheduled meetings	3	24.7	2	26.9
Further contacts	18	27.8	40	25.5
Other	2	4.8	2	13.1

Table 6.8   Communication episodes of German and British site managers over total observation

| Communication episodes | German | | British | |
	av. no./day	% of working time	av. no./day	% of working time
With bosses	1	1.1	6	4.1
With peers	9	20.4	12	10.9
With subs	20	27.4	30	17.8
With outsiders	2	10.5	2	0.4
Mixed	1	18.5	3	31.0

The data show that both managers spent more time communicating than in our other pair comparisons, but the difference between the site and the packaging managers was only a small one. Otherwise the patterns of activities and communication episodes were more similar than in our other pair comparisons. It seems that the core technology of unit production was the overriding influence. However, we must stress, that these data can at best be *illustrative* because of the limited period of observation and the fact that the number of comparisons was so small.

SUMMARY

Our review has shown that the managers' jobs in each of the three paired companies, although chosen to be as comparable as possible, still had considerable differences. We illustrated this by taking pairs of jobs that were the most comparable amongst those we studied, but even so there were considerable differences. In the breweries these came mainly from the much more diverse market served by the German brewery. In life assurance it came from the much more regulated market in Germany compared with the more varied products of the British company. Perhaps partly because of this the German company also differed in its much more highly developed use of information technology which had to a great extent reduced the tasks to be performed by the middle managers. Yet another difference in the German company was its much more integrated organization, which reduced the need for coordination. In comparing the two construction companies, it seems that the nature of their industry, that of one-off production, overshadowed other differences.

We compared the activities and contact pattern of the most comparable pairs of managers in each industry against our expectations of differences, but the limitations of the data in terms of time of observation and numbers of people mean that these are only of illustrative interest.

In this chapter we have sought to put the findings presented in earlier chapters against the background of earlier studies. With regard to a number of structural characteristics, for example, the higher degree of formalization or greater decentralization in British organizations or the wider spans of control and the flatter hierarchies in the German organizations, our cases correspond to the findings of previous studies of a comparative nature, as does the fact that German middle managers in general do not have a budget.

We have also identified the ways in which the middle managers' jobs in each of the paired companies differed because of their contextual or organizational differences. We identified some differences which would influence the tasks that the managers had to perform and the ways in which they behaved. It seems clear that any cross-cultural comparison must be muddied by contextual and organizational differences.

7 Management and Institutions

National institutions set certain constraints on the available choices for organizations and their incumbents. But the nature of the institutions are themselves the products of cultural choices, preferences and biases:

> Germany is an ordered and orderly society, one in which there are laws and systems for most aspects of economic life. The preparation and development of people for management is no exception.[1]

This chapter will focus on the institutional explanations for the differences observed between managers in the two countries. The distinction between this chapter and the next, on cultural explanations, is in some ways artificial. After all, institutions are built by people conditioned by the same education and life experience. They enshrine and perpetuate many of the shared values of a society. This chapter, however, will deal with values embodied in institutions, systems and frameworks (educational, legal, industrial, organizational).

What follows is a selective exploration of institutional differences between the two countries. The intention is to highlight those institutional influences which seem to shed light on the actions or attitudes of the managers observed:

> Management is not a phenomenon that can be isolated from other processes taking place in a society ... It interacts with what happens in the family, at school, in politics, and government.[2]

THE LAW OF THE LAND

In Germany, there are regulations and decrees governing most aspects of everyday life and the 'rule of order and the law', *Rechtsstaat*, is often emphasized. Germany even has fail-safe laws which come into operation should the existing laws become unen-forceable (*Notstandsgesetze*). Britain does not even have a written constitution or legal code. Legal systems are based on custom, inference and negotiation. English common law, for instance, is based on the notion of precedent, rather than constructed and laid down by legal scholars and writers.

In comparison with Britain, Germany is a low discretion society. There are fewer grey areas in which to manoeuvre, and there is less call for personal influence or compromise. In Britain, it is safe to assume that anything not forbidden is allowed, whereas in Germany, it is more likely to be the other way round.

A similar pattern emerges in the legislation governing mergers and acquisitions. The takeover regulations in Britain are notoriously flexible by EC, and particularly German, standards. In Germany, hostile takeovers are not well-received. The former chairman of the Deutsche Bank, Alfred Herrhausen, has been an outspoken but fairly typical critic of takeovers conducted in aggressive US fashion. As he sees it, 'Such conduct has no place in our economic culture.'[3]

For this reason, Britain has served as something of a training ground for hostile takeovers since the mid-1980s. Growth in British companies has been primarily through mergers, rather than organi-cally driven through expanding activities by direct investment in capital equipment. About three out of every four British companies have acquired or been acquired in the past five years.[4]

The repercussions of all this activity have been two-fold for the managers we observed. First, it has had a direct impact on company structures and therefore on the job responsibilities of the managers. The less haphazard organic growth of German companies has made for a pattern of more integrated production units. The British companies, have found it more difficult to integrate functions. It follows that the British companies in our study required their managers to engage in more cross-over meetings of the steering committee, working party and project group variety. Coordination was not built-in to the structure, as it was in the German companies, and therefore had to happen in specific forums.

The second impact on managerial jobs and behaviour is more subtle and a direct causal link is more difficult to establish. It relates to time-orientation. The vulnerability to hostile takeover forces British company boards to concentrate on profits now rather than investment for the future. For example, the need to maintain dividends partly explains the reduced investment in research and development in Britain:

Between 1981 and 1985, British firms spent £250 per annum per employee, compared with £400 in West Germany.[5]

The priority given to shareholder value means that British chief executives may find themselves forced to take quick-fix measures in order to satisfy institutional investors.

These decisions, together with the short-term ethos they promote, inevitably permeate the organization. While a link is difficult to prove, there was evidence of short-termism in our British companies. It manifested itself, for instance, in the ubiquitous willingness to 'tinker' with corporate structures, and to reshuffle responsibilities, at all levels. It also showed in the everyday actions of managers. They would refer to 'back of the envelope' planning or solutions. Solutions which were expedient were considered appropriate.

The more legalistic orientation of German society is also apparent within organizations. For instance, it is no coincidence that German companies employ, proportionately, two-and-a-half times as many lawyers as British companies.[6] Law, after engineering and economics, is an important subject for would-be managers. The law graduates are not evenly spread throughout industry. They tend to congregate in commerce, banking and finance, rather than heavy industry. They also tend to favour particular functions, notably personnel. Quite a number of German personnel managers have a law degree and a personnel director may even have a doctorate in law.[7] This, in part, reflects the more legalistic nature of personnel work in Germany compared with that in Britain:

> The German personnel manager is to a much higher degree engaged in applying the law in the company – law on conditions, safety, worker representation, and so on.[8]

MANAGEMENT AND WORKERS

The patterns that prevail in the legal systems of Britain and Germany are echoed in the systems of labour–management relations. In Germany these have been codified in detail, while attempts to do so in Britain have never succeeded. British managers continue to rely on a system based on horse-trading, muddling through and personal relations with the worker representatives and shop stewards. British companies are replete with informal understandings between workers and management, established by long-standing custom.[9]

The degree of integration of employees in general and the trade unions in particular into corporate structures has had a positive influence on the business culture in Germany.[10] In some industries, such as steel and mining, trade unions have a direct input into the corporate decision-making process, because they have a member in the board of CEOs (*Arbeitsdirektor*), who are in charge of the personnel function. In other industries, for instance the car industry, there are representatives of the employees, the number of which varies with the size of the company, on the supervisory board. Despite a climate becoming more and more rough, employers and trade unions have, so far, referred to themselves not in adversarial terms ('us and them') but as partners (*Sozialpartner*).

The organization of trade unions in Germany is very different from that in Britain. There are sixteen large unions in Germany, one for each major 'industry'. The fact that they are *industrial* unions means that they encompass all types and grades of employees in a given sector. Thus, some of the middle managers in our study were covered by the collective bargaining agreements for more junior staff. These agreements cover pay and hours worked which, in the German companies, meant that some of the middle managers also clocked on and off. This helps to explain why German middle managers tended readily to identify downwards and to try to play down status differentials with their subordinates. A typical response when asked how they wished to be seen by their subordinates: 'I want to be viewed as a normal employee, not as a superior' (Accounting manager, German insurance company).

The fact that the German unions are sector-specific impinged on the work of the managers observed in another way. It meant that demarcation disputes were technically impossible. In fact, there is no phrase in German for demarcation dispute. Another practical implication was that German production managers had more scope to move workers around in answer to short-term manning needs.

The British trade unions are much more fragmented along trade and hierarchical lines than the German ones. Inevitably, this creates tension within companies. The archetypal division is that between the production and maintenance functions in manufacturing industry. Three of the five British brewery managers were involved in demarcation disputes or concerns during the observation. This is more likely to happen in a recessionary environment. Trades become very protective of their special responsibilities and especially sensitive to erosion of tasks. The maintenance workers in the brewery, for instance, caused a stir about the workers in packaging hijacking one of their tasks. The matter was resolved in a special meeting between the two heads of function.

The British system is also much less formalized than the German one. The shop-stewards might come to see the manager at any time, not just in a specific forum or by appointment. Consequently, there is a lot more arbitration and involvement for the British managers. Negotiating with the unions was a preoccupation for a number of the managers observed and a high premium was placed on their ability to handle these negotiations. The job description of the British brewery's packaging manager spells out the dimensions of this burden in a 'highly pressurised industrial relations context':

> Continually dealing with shop-floor representatives, directly or through supervisory staff. Discussions with stewards require persuasion and tact since any misunderstanding or misstatement may have long-term effects on the operation and efficiency of the department and the site as a whole.

While this job represents the extreme of British managerial involvement with the unions, unions were a recurring preoccupation during the observation. It was no coincidence that three of the fifteen British managers observed were themselves former shop-stewards.

In contrast, the German middle managers had very low involvement with the unions. German trade unions have little direct influence in the workplace. Where German middle managers have formal dealings with the workers, it will be through the works council. Here, relations tend to be formalized and regulated. Strikes and lockouts are a legitimate means of applying pressure in collective bargaining, but not in the exercise of codetermination, consultation and information rights in the workplace, where only peaceful negotiations are permitted:

> The works council has no right to strike and extensive juridification helps to channel and depoliticize industrial conflict and also encourages the professionalization of conflict management.[11]

Again, there is little ambiguity or need for negotiation. Everyone knows what is expected. The law defines precisely the questions on which councils have rights of information, consultation and codetermination.

In Britain, there is no institutionalized system of industrial democracy at company level in the private or public sector. The nearest any of the British companies had to the German system of codetermination were the joint consultative committees in the brewery. However, these were only devoted to consultation and the dissemination of information, and gave workers no codecision or veto rights.

Although British workers lag some way behind their German counterparts in terms of formal rights, it has been argued that there is little difference in terms of their actual influence – particularly where the organization of work and pay are concerned.[12] But the fact that industrial democracy is not institutionalized in Britain has meant that influence has been achieved at a high cost, in terms of disruption of industrial production. Inevitably it has been Britain's middle managers who have had to contend with and try to settle such disruption.

Thus, conflict is inherent in the British model while in the German one it is 'designed' out. Yet, the German model is not without its drawbacks. From the point of view of the German middle managers, the codetermination system inhibits, among other things, rapid decision-making and action with regard to personnel. It makes decision-making what Calori and Lawrence have termed 'more conditional'.[13]

For instance, when British managers want to re-route their budget, make changes in short-time or overtime work, or on personnel matters, they are not heavily impeded. British companies are organized in a way that facilitates rapid action. According to our findings, British managers tend to have more discretion in spending and personnel policy – redesigning jobs, hiring and firing, regrading, and training – without lengthy discussions upwards or sideways with the personnel department.

Thus, British partiality to 'back-of-the-envelope' planning and expedient solutions (mentioned earlier), has an institutional, as well as perhaps a cultural, explanation. The prevailing system of industrial relations does not just influence what middle managers do; it also colours what they view as possible. It shapes the managerial mindset.

PREPARING MANAGERS

In Chapter 3, we described the education and training institutions in Britain and Germany. Here we shall consider how the orientation and ethos of those different systems may have influenced the behaviour or attitudes of the middle managers in our study.

The majority of the German middle managers in our study had completed an apprenticeship – either a technical or a commercial one. Apprenticeships form the backbone of vocational training in all economic sectors, and high numbers of technical, commercial, supervisory and managerial staff have served them. It is a system which cuts across the shop-floor and the office. Inevitably, this provides a consistency of experience and outlook among employees of different grades and functions, which is uncommon in Britain.

In addition to technical knowledge and skills, apprentices learn about costs, design, and the planning and administration of production. There is exposure to a wide variety of work situations and problem-solving tasks. The apprenticeship always ends in a theoretical examination and a practical skill-based test, and successful completion confers the legally protected status of *Facharbeiter* (skilled worker). About two-thirds of the German worker population possess this certificate, including some company directors. In comparison, two-thirds of the working population in Britain have no occupational qualification at all.[14]

Besides the direct impact on the managers themselves of serving an apprenticeship, there is also the effect that it has on workers. The actions and attitudes of middle managers cannot be isolated from that of their 'charges'. For instance, the apprenticeship system may help to explain why German workers require less supervision, and why German structures can be more integrated (see previous chapter).

The apprenticeship also helps to instil occupational pride. This has some important repercussions. With intrinsic pride in their work, the onus on the manager to motivate workers is reduced, and the manager's ability to handle workers is not so important. Thus the British emphasis on 'man-management' can, in part, be given an institutional explanation.

The highly skilled and responsible German workers do not necessarily need a manager, American-style, to 'motivate' them. They expect their boss to be a Meister to assign their tasks and to be the expert in resolving technical problems.[15]

On completing their apprenticeship, a number of the German managers in our study had gone on to attend *Fachhochschulen* (polytechnics). Again, these are institutions which are marked by a strong vocational slant. The *Fachhochschulen* are well-integrated with industry, not only in their avowed and evident practicality, but also in their lecturing staff. Lecturers are required by law to be university graduates and to have a minimum of five years' industrial experience. This requirement facilitates the integration of theory and practice. It bears witness to thoughtful design and to the more-codified German system.

Even those German managers in our study who opted for the academic, as opposed to the vocational, route into industry, had a specific training. German university graduates in management have invariably studied a subject which is directly related to their future careers in business. For instance, the German brewing company recruited its managers in the production area exclusively among graduates in biochemistry or brewing and a doctorate has even more cachet. Furthermore, graduates are not just recruited on the strength of their degree subject but, to a large extent, for the specific content of their courses. Indeed, candidates may well be quizzed on the elective subjects they chose and their presumptive relevance to the company's operations.[16]

In comparison, the particular specialism of a British university graduate is of less interest to prospective employers. The ability to reach degree standard is seen as promising a general level of intellectual ability and learning capacity. Even companies with quite precise technical needs will cast their nets wide. For instance, an article in *The Independent* cited the recruitment manager for IBM as saying that the annual graduate intake consisted of about 36 per cent from 'any discipline'. It is a lead which comes from the top – Sir Anthony Cleaver, then chairman of IBM UK Holdings, has a degree in classics.[17]

In Britain, then, opting for an arts degree is not the career death-knell that it would be in German industry. By European standards Britain produces large numbers of arts graduates and companies are unusually receptive to the skills they have to offer. Indeed, some British firms actively encourage recruits with arts or humanities backgrounds. For example, the national recruitment partner for Touche Ross, the accountancy firm, commented:

> If you can pick the right arts graduates, then they tend to do very well – sometimes better than those with a more vocational degree because they often have better communicative skills and a command of the language.[18]

Such a comment from a German employer is almost unthinkable. The observation is indicative of the British conception of management as socially complex, rather than a technical or intellectual challenge. It reflects the high esteem placed on a generalism and is echoed in the backgrounds of those at the top. As Lane observed:

> Generally, it remains true to say that the promotion to top-level posts of 'gifted amateurs' remains a uniquely British phenomenon.[19]

This British bias towards generalists and towards plurality of background has its drawbacks. Simply stated it means that the route into management is poorly signposted. It is for this reason that many aspiring managers opt for the surrogate path of accountancy. Accountancy provides a guaranteed entry *into* management, even if it does not prepare the individual *for* management.

This somewhat *ad hoc* initiation to management is also visible at lower levels. Certain educational credentials are preferred, but there is not an agreed 'best way'. This accounts for the rather haphazard mix of pre-entry qualifications among the British managers in our study (see Chapter 3). Compared with that in Germany, the British education system is not well geared to the needs of industry. It is also difficult to characterize. Its chief feature is probably its heterogeneity.

The German system espouses a technical and specific ethos. The educational and vocational training systems are highly codified, and they fit neatly into the highly regulated work environment. For instance, most positions in the hierarchy will have a fixed qualification attached to them.

Improving Managers

While management development is not a physical institution in the sense of an organization or body, it is an established practice. There is a conventional wisdom about the best way of developing a manager, and that wisdom differs between nations.

In Britain (as in the USA) much trouble is taken over career routes to produce general managers. Those earmarked as high-flyers are likely to be exposed to a variety of functions in an attempt to broaden their skills and vision:

> The generalist notion of management development is most rooted in the Anglo-Saxon culture ... Around the age of thirty, the human resource management problem is to identify those individuals who have 'potential', usually synonymous with some notion of generalist or general management potential.[20]

This is not the pattern in Germany where managers tend to follow strictly functional routes upwards, typically in a particular industry and sometimes in a single company. While British managers tend to follow upward spirals, their German counterparts tend to climb up functional chimneys:

> Promotion in the German enterprise follows this functionally specialized route and retraining across functions is relatively rare.[21]

The two approaches are characterized in Figures 7.1 and 7.2.

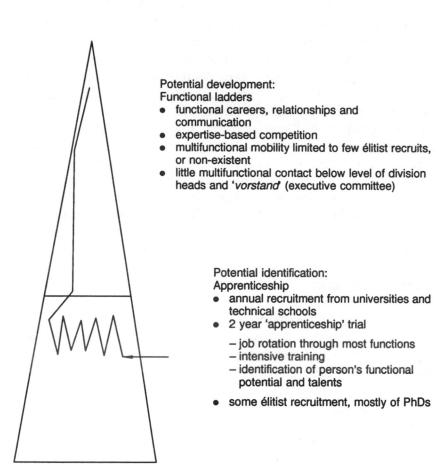

Potential development:
Functional ladders
- functional careers, relationships and communication
- expertise-based competition
- multifunctional mobility limited to few élitist recruits, or non-existent
- little multifunctional contact below level of division heads and '*vorstand*' (executive committee)

Potential identification:
Apprenticeship
- annual recruitment from universities and technical schools
- 2 year 'apprenticeship' trial
  - job rotation through most functions
  - intensive training
  - identification of person's functional potential and talents
- some élitist recruitment, mostly of PhDs

Source: Evans >et al.[22] (Reproduced with permission.)

Figure 7.1 Functional approach to management development: the 'Germanic' model

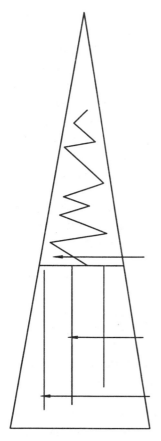

Potential development
Managed potential development
- careful monitoring of high potentials by
  management review committees
- review to match up performance and potential
  with short- and long-term job and development
  requirements
- importance of management development staff

Potential identification:
Unmanaged functional trial
- little elite recruitment
- decentralized recruitment for technical or
  functional jobs
- 5–7 years' trial
- no corporate monitoring
- problem of internal "potential identification" via
  assessments, assessment centers, indicators
- possible complementary recruitment of high
  potentials

Source: Evans *et al.*[22] (Reproduced with permission.)

Figure 7.2 Managed development approach to management development:
the 'Anglo–Dutch' model

COMPARISON OF THE ANGLO-DUTCH AND GERMANIC MODELS OF MANAGEMENT DEVELOPMENT

The German preference is clearly for specialists whose power-base is expertise. British companies try to create generalists whose strength is their adaptability. It follows that the British companies did not just rotate managers more often; they also had many more 'general management' positions which also served as developmental posts for aspiring senior managers. In contrast, the German companies were singularly lacking in such posts. Even the chief executives in the

German companies had specific functional responsibilities to discharge.

Institutional patterns therefore served to shape and reinforce the self-identity of both sets of managers. Whereas the British middle managers interviewed gave themselves the broad label 'manager', the German ones tended to describe themselves as functional specialists – *Kaufmann* or *Techniker*. The Germans did not distinguish between the technical and managerial aspects of their job in the same way as the British managers. The British, not only distinguished, but gave them different status, and regarded them as mutually exclusive:

> Unique to Britain seems to be the implicit belief that, having crossed over, you can't look back, as though the boundary to the portals of management was the River Styx itself.[23]

All this reflects a very different conception of what management is about and what managers require to do their jobs better. In Germany, promotion is about accumulating expertise, and gaining total mastery of one's job. A knowledge and understanding of the work to be done at all levels is a prerequisite to advancement.

In Britain, promotion has more to do with demonstrating one's managerial potential – in terms of handling people, getting the best out of them and showing breadth of vision. British managers get appraised, promoted and gain status from doing the strictly managerial things right. In Britain it is all right not to master the whole technical job, provided one has the people-management skills. This is seen as the middle management task *par excellence* – with responsibilities for strategy, finance and marketing tending to fall to top management. It is because management, the activity, is seen as socially, rather than technically complex, that management, the body of knowledge, is seen as transferable.

In Britain, successful management is based on the elusive faculty, judgement. This demands sensitivity to other people, to their motivation and their likely commitment to a course of action. The manager also has to be in tune with the prevailing mood so as to find the right time to say or do something.

Judgement is also about understanding priorities; about discriminating between the issues which are competing for managerial attention. Individuals may be born with common sense, but managerial judgement is honed by exposure to diverse experiences. As the marketing manager in the British insurance company, put it:

You've got to go over the hot coals. The more scar tissue you accumulate, the better tooled up you are for the next job. You're more relaxed, you've seen it before and you feel able to handle things.

Germans are more concerned with technical skills – these can be taught very readily by those who know to those who do not. Britons are more concerned with human skills. They can best be learnt by experience and helped by advice and reflection, and by mentoring or coaching.

British managers are readier to believe that they can learn from others. This is reflected in the greater participation in management programmes and in a greater interest in improving their managerial as distinct from their technical competence. This openness to external input is perhaps seen at its most extreme by the insurance manager who welcomed visiting students from Brighton Polytechnic, not for what he might impart to them or for the opportunity to enhance his status in the community, but for what he might learn *from* them – in terms of the naive questions they would ask.

In Anglo-Saxon countries, then, management is seen as a never-ending learning process. Why? Because management is about people, not about the finite knowledge associated with structures or production processes. As Hannaway sees Anglo-Saxon management:

> Success in business is more dependent upon relating effectively with people than solving scholastic puzzles with numbers or words.[24]

MANAGEMENT AS AN INSTITUTION

In Germany, until recently, there has been less writing, thinking, and talking about management *per se*. Germans have a much weaker conviction that there is something separate, definable, and objective called management. They doubt that one can really extrapolate this aspect of a variety of tasks and label it separately, make generalizations about it, offer exhortations concerning it – and provide a disembodied, generalized training in it. The Anglo-Saxon concept of management as a unified profession is not widely accepted. Executive staff see themselves primarily as specialists in a certain field.

This German orientation is reflected in attitudes and institutions: it can be seen in the paucity of indigeneous classical management literature, in the relative immunity to American management thought, and in the absence of undergraduate courses in management or MBAs – as well as the low numbers of Germans who attend business schools abroad, compared with other national contingents.

These institutional differences have a direct impact on the attitudes and behaviour of managers. German managers, for instance, have a much more specific understanding of management: one does a specific job, does not change industry, applies a specific knowledge and training, uses particularist job titles, not general ones such as manager or executive. All this has an important influence on careers, and on attitudes to, and the reality of, inter-company mobility.

German managers, then, espouse a culture of mastery: initially this is based on technical expertise – being the best clerk. But the basis for the expertise changes as managers move up the hierarchy. Expert power in the form of technical know-how gives way to expert power as embodied by doctorates and qualifications. In the higher reaches of management, it is not possible to 'prove' one's expertise as it is at middle-management level – so it has to be taken on trust and ability as certified by academic qualifications.

These separate orientations colour what managers find satisfying about their jobs. So, as we saw in Chapter 4, when describing their jobs, Germans focus on the technical tasks. They enjoy the operational side of their jobs and regret when they do not find time for it. In Britain, there is a more pronounced split between the careers of the technical expert and that of the manager. British managers see the core of their job as managerial. They attach more importance to delegation and do not expect to be involved in technical work. As one of the British insurance managers put it: 'If you have a dog, why bark yourself?'

8 Management and Value Systems

Starting from descriptions of observed behaviour, we have offered a variety of explanations for the differences between British and German managers. These explanations have ranged from individual differences in function, career and educational background, to contextual differences in technology, management systems, organizational structure, and institutions. Having considered these, it makes it easier to explore the possible cultural explanations for the differences we found in managers' views and behaviour.

Managers in Britain and Germany hold different sets of values which give them different perspectives and lead to different ways of behaving. These value systems have an impact on motivation, satisfaction, patterns of interaction and so on. They can be likened to lenses through which experience is interpreted and action is guided – and because all information is processed via these lenses, individuals are only dimly aware of the peculiarities of their value systems. It often takes an outsider, with a different set of values, to expose that which is taken for granted.

Yet this is not a straightforward exercise, for two reasons: first, because the researchers themselves are also culturally blinkered in their interpretation of behaviour. As Bertrand Russell pointed out, tongue-in-cheek:

Animals studied by Americans rush about frantically, with an incredible display of hustle and pep, and at last achieve the desired result by chance. Animals observed by Germans sit and think, and at last evolve the solution out of their inner consciousness.[1]

In our own study, we tried to remove our cultural blinkers through joint observation, where possible together, otherwise sequentially, by a researcher from one country, then by one from the other country. Inevitably, some cultural bias still colours our interpretation.

The second difficulty is that national culture is not a 'clean' category which can simply be isolated. It is difficult to disentangle which shared values are driven by the organization and which are societal. Nor does national culture declare itself openly. Rather it manifests itself obliquely in organizational behaviour, and is crystallized in organizational structures and national institutions. It is therefore impossible to put forward cultural explanations without referring back to some of the structural and institutional explanations discussed in earlier chapters. There is a circuitous relationship between individuals, organizations and institutions. As Laurent expressed it:

> Managers from different national cultures hold different assumptions about the nature of management, authority, structure, and organizational relationships. These assumptions shape different value systems and get translated into different management practices, which in turn reinforce the original assumptions.[2]

In tackling the issue of national culture, the only broad framework available is that provided by Geert Hofstede,[3] a Dutch psychologist. The following chapter therefore relies heavily on Hofstede's framework to categorize the cultural differences observed; but it also draws on the work of other writers who have commented more specifically on organizational differences between Britain and Germany.

In an attempt to limit the number of variable factors, Hofstede conducted his research among employees at a variety of levels in subsidiaries of the same multinational corporation in forty countries. From the results, he identified four cultural dimensions on which countries could be plotted. These dimensions were:

- 'individualism/collectivism';
- 'uncertainty avoidance';
- 'power distance',
- 'masculinity/feminity'.

He went on to argue that these four dimensions determined the way in which organizations were structured and managed.

Hofstede's research was helpful to the present study in two ways: first, it established a well-defined and empirically based terminology to describe national cultures; second, the large sample size provided a broader base to some of our findings which would otherwise be too tentative. In return, the present study supplies evidence gleaned from observation, thus helping to validate Hofstede's speculative arguments regarding the influence of cultural factors on organizations and organizational behaviour.

Of the four dimensions, only two, Hofstede found, show marked differences between Britain and Germany (uncertainty avoidance and individualism). A third (power distance), was interesting for the very reason that Britain and Germany unexpectedly recorded identical low scores. Only the masculinity dimension – on which the two countries also scored equally – was not deemed particularly relevant to the present study.

HANDLING THE UNKNOWN

Societies respond to uncertainty in different ways, some by cultivating a laid-back or fatalistic approach to life, while others strive to reduce this uncertainty with a miscellany of planning, procedures, and contingency arrangements. On Hofstede's scale of 0 (high tolerance) to 100 (low tolerance), British comfort with uncertainty was far greater (35) than German (65).

The German managers' desire for control over uncertainty manifested itself in many ways during our research. It showed up in the contrasting organization structures, career patterns and approaches to management development; in the different bases of managerial authority, views of change and everyday management relations; and of course, in the institutions such as the legal framework and labour–management relations.

During our research, German antipathy towards uncertainty first became apparent in resistance to observation. German managers needed more comforting than their British counterparts about what the exercise would involve, about which aspects were being recorded, and about what would be done with the results. German managers were less likely to agree to observation at short notice. If it had not been arranged three months ago and did not have the personal endorsement of their boss, they would not be cajoled into it. In a couple of extreme cases, even when observation days had been agreed, the German managers subsequently changed their minds.

Even with all these reassurances, the observation exercise remains unpredictable – that is, susceptible to unplanned interruptions or emergencies. So, while the German managers were at ease in their own controlled environment, they were less happy being shadowed around the company – they often wanted to check with colleagues that it would be all right.

British managers are comfortable with uncertainty. When they refer to 'back of the envelope' planning or solutions this suggests a quick and practical solution. British managers are often more concerned about being expeditious than achieving perfection. As one construction manager explained to his boss in a meeting: 'I did it at the traffic lights on the way in.' This jokey comment was meant to show that it was not a fully worked-out solution – but it did not have negative connotations about the subordinate's time-organization or conscientiousness.

British management places a premium on improvization and resourcefulness. Managing 'on the hoof', 'thinking on your feet', these are the skills that managers feel they need to cope with their work, which they readily describe as juggling or plate-spinning.

The argument is reversible for the Germans. There is an expectation of reliability and punctuality in everyday life just as there is in business, a feeling that without rules, life would become anarchic. There is an emphasis on planning and purposefully sticking to those plans which is both a strength (long-termism) and a weakness (inflexibility).

German managers do not like to be caught 'on the hop'. Lawrence refers to 'the almost neurotic desire to have reserves, stocks, protection, something to fall back on; if they never run out of anything it must be Germany.'[4]

Degrees of Formality

One recurrent difference between the managers in the two countries was the degree of interpersonal formality in the German workplace. The existence of certain rituals and the heavier patterning of communication is another facet of uncertainty avoidance. This showed through in a number of ways.

German discomfort with uncertainty showed up in more ritualized face-to-face exchanges, than in Britain. German colleagues are careful to greet each other properly in the morning and evening and also at mid-day with *Mahlzeit*, when they go to lunch.

In German organizations, managers set limits and boundaries as to how close they wish to be with a colleague. The polite, '*Sie*', form of address, can be useful for the purposes of self-protection. It helps to indicate how far one is prepared to have contact with another person and makes explicit the nature or maturity of a relationship. To '*siezen*' someone indicates respect or insufficient acquaintance, whereas to '*duzen*' someone denotes being on first-name terms – and is the exception rather than the rule. The transition from the polite to the familiar form is usually the product of much *angst* and deliberation. It is not a decision that is taken lightly since the offer to put the relationship on a less-formal footing can always be turned down.

In Britain, of course, there is no such distinction between forms of address. The straightforward pronoun 'you' is a great leveller. It can be used without having to worry about generation gaps or differences in status or hierarchy. Having a single form of address for everyone means that the problem of establishing the nature of a relationship is actually displaced. In Britain, authority, deference, respect or friendliness are conveyed in more subtle ways: in patterns of speech, choice of vocabulary, attitude and body language. These are much more ambiguous signals than the unmistakable familiar/polite distinction.

German managers are also more inclined to use formal titles, especially *Doktor*. Even long-standing colleagues are likely to address each other by their title and surname, 'Herr Direktor Braun' or 'Frau Doktor Strauss'. This does reflect status-consciousness – British managers are every bit as status-conscious, but in a less formalized way. In Britain, much more is inferred from tone of speech. Britain is a high-context culture compared to Germany. What passes for informality in Britain, then, is just a more complex and less formalized code.

Another manifestation of the relative tolerance for ambiguity and uncertainty can be seen in the different uses of humour. Having hypothesized that the two countries might differ in their recourse to humour, both sets of managers were asked whether they ever used humour. Both sets of managers responded that they did. But in the later interviews, the explicit reference to humour was dropped, and the question was changed to 'How would you ease relationships?' When unprompted, the German managers made no reference to humour, while several of their British counterparts cited humour as an essential means of easing relationships:

I would try to keep things fairly light-hearted – I think it is a useful way of team-building. You try to create a reasonably relaxed atmosphere perhaps by taking the mickey out of someone, not rudely or unfairly, but in a way I know they will be able to accept. (New Business Manager, British insurance company)

There is nothing wrong with people smiling and laughing as far as I am concerned. I will joke with them and vice versa – whilst at the same time trying to make sure that we work on the particular problem or come up with a solution. (Existing Business Manager, British insurance company)

Humour, depending on who the person is. I feel easier with the people who understand my humour. Some people are better with humour than others. (Surrenders Manager, British insurance company)

I try to relax people, particularly auditees because they are always nervous. You have to try immediately to break the ice otherwise you will not get anything out of them and they will not be any good either. An auditor can feel when people need calming down or whatever – crack a joke, smile, be pleasant and as soon as you know they are relaxed, you can start. (Quality Manager, British construction company)

Is there a way of accounting for the inconsistency in the German responses compared with the consistency among the British managers? One explanation is that German managers are not expected to be humorous. Nevertheless humour is considered useful and legitimate in so far as it contributes to the *Arbeitsklima* (working environment), thereby supporting the high task-orientation which characterizes the German companies. Only in this respect is humour exploited by German middle managers:

I have the feeling that one has to use humour and has to be friendly. You will get more out of people this way than telling them 'that's what you have to do, and [if] you don't do it, you will see what will happen'. (Packaging manager, German brewery)

The difference, in Britain, is that managers will often use humour deliberately to 'get things done'. Humour, from the British perspective, is a legitimate managerial tool. This was especially noticeable during the observation phase.

Contrary to popular belief, the German managers observed were neither dour or humourless, but they were unlikely to employ humour in the ambiguous way favoured by the British managers – using 'jokes' to convey messages. British managers were more likely to take a tactical view of humour.

In Britain, humour is routinely injected into most mundane requests to cancel any hint of authoritarianism. It is seen as the quickest way to connect with someone. It takes the edge off a brusque instruction and helps managers to sell unilateral decisions. It all makes gaining compliance easier. Consider the following tactical uses:

- *To criticize a subordinate* the regional director of the British construction company teases a long-winded subordinate in a meeting, declaring incredulously, 'he hasn't drawn breath for five minutes'.
- *To communicate more memorably* one insurance administration manager expresses his delegation philosophy thus: 'I want to give you enough rope to do the job well, but not enough to hang me.'
- *To discharge tension* the proposed restructuring, in the British brewery, of the system of sick pay set management in opposition to the trade unions. The shop-stewards put forward a completely unrealistic proposal. The personnel manager tapped out some figures on his calculator, then announced apologetically: 'I am sorry, I can only get eight digits on my adding machine.' The point was made without antagonizing the shop-stewards and bringing negotiations to a halt.
- *To diffuse criticism* to ward off criticism about his report being not especially useful, one construction manager explained: 'It was either this or make paper planes.'
- *To soften a blow* rather than coldly turning down a subordinate's request for an upholstered chair, the contracts manager tells him: 'It is too comfy. You would just go to sleep in it.' Another contracts manager sells a change of job-responsibilities to a subordinate by telling him, 'I have got some good news for you – if you like hard work.'
- *Interfunctional rivalry* on receiving no answer from their colleagues in the commercial department, one technical manager tells his subordinates: 'I forgot, they (the quantity surveyors) work Mickey Mouse hours.' Deriding other groups serves as a team-bonding device and reinforces group identity.

Although these examples demonstrate the British penchant for persuasion as a management style, they also reflect a comfort with ambiguity. Humour is a way of delivering criticism with a smile, of singling out bad behaviour while confirming a sense of belonging, of challenging authority without appearing to do so. Humour is used as a channel for making oblique statements which avoid head-on assertion. It is the natural instrument of ambiguity.

Managers' Expectations of Others

The different attitudes to uncertainty were also evident in the expectations that each set of managers had of other people. For instance, there was a marked difference in expectations of subordinates. The British managers consistently emphasized energetic qualities: commitment, initiative, ownership, responsibility and honesty – especially in terms of reporting bad news as well as good. As the technical manager in the British insurance company put it: 'I want to see a willingness to accept responsibility and a readiness to own up to mistakes.'

The German managers had comparatively straightforward expectations of their subordinates. They tended to want consistency and order rather than personal drive or enthusiasm. The German managers attached more importance to trust, dependability, and punctuality as a basis for a good relationship between managers and subordinates. One of the German construction managers simply expected his subordinates to do a quality job: *'ordentlich, exakt, fehlerlos, korrekt arbeiten'* ('to work orderly, accurately, faultlessly and properly'). Such expectations would seem a touch naive and old-fashioned coming from a British manager.

In Germany, then, dependability is seen as the cornerstone of efficiency. In particular, German managers are sticklers for punctuality. This was regularly stressed by the German managers interviewed whereas it was not once mentioned by British managers. These different attitudes were confirmed during the observation phase.

In Britain, there was far more tolerance for lateness. This was epitomized by one construction manager who went out into the corridor at 10.10 in order to enquire, 'When and where is the 10 o'clock meeting?' Or again, in the British brewery, the Brewing and Fermenting manager completely forgot to turn up for one meeting. He received a call thirty minutes later to point out his gaffe but he was not unduly perturbed or apologetic.

As a rule, lateness did not elicit direct criticism in Britain. Often, it would provoke no more than a raised eyebrow, a 'tut-tut' or a mock reprimand. For instance, one of the brewery managers arrived late to a brainstorming session with some of his peers. The leader of the session commented, 'You realize we are going to have to punish you for this?' Another colleague added enthusiastically, 'And I shall be the one to administer it.'

Meetings tended to overrun, so that managers might say at the start: 'I've got to get away by . . .' This relaxed view of punctuality may stem from the fact that Britons view management as continuous and unpredictable – not something that can easily be batched and handled in fixed time-slots.

A further twist to the British view of punctuality is that it is relative. For instance, there are meetings when managers make sure they are on time, and others where punctuality is considered less important. This was particularly in evidence in the British construction industry where managers spent a lot of time 'on the road' visiting sites. In order to be on time for every meeting, managers would have to allow buffers of up to half an hour. But they made this effort if the site meeting involved the client.

Punctuality is also relative in terms of hierarchy: the lateness of a boss, in Britain, is more tolerated than that of a subordinate. In Germany, the reverse was more likely to be true. German middle managers want to set an example to their subordinates and so they always try to be on time.

The greater delineation of time by German managers is also reflected in the boundary between work and leisure. The German approach to work is quite transactional. Once at their desks, the managers use their time to the full, stopping little for the socialization that is so much a part of British office life. German managers work in the workplace and relax at home. John Mole observed:

There is a strong sense that the relationship between the company and the employee is contractual. You are paid for so many hours and you work as hard as you can, but that is the end of it.[5]

For the British managers observed there was far more overlap between work and leisure. They were more likely to engage in private-cum-social activities during working hours – shopping, visits to the dentist, banking, drinking, personal phone calls were all witnessed during the course of the observation. This less stringent view of work was noted by a German manager with IBM:

Dieter Schultz, a German manager with IBM in Portsmouth, took up his post as product manager in 1986 and found that most lunch-times and particularly on Fridays the vast majority of his management team decamped to the pub. 'I stopped that right away', he says. 'Now they are not allowed off the premises. It did not make me very popular at the time but it is not good for efficiency. There is no way we could do that in Germany. No way.[6]

According to Hofstede, the higher work intensity in the German companies further corroborates the desire for certainty:

> For strong uncertainty-avoidance countries, working hard is caused by an inner urge – it is a way of relieving stress.[7]

While the British managers were less sustained in their output than their German counterparts, they were also likely to work late, to take work home with them, and might even drop into the office/factory/site at the weekend. In Germany, home life is more jealously guarded, and it is unusual to find a German middle manager who is willing to take work home or arrange a business meeting outside working hours:

> Germans have a strong sense of privacy and their protective shell extends much further into public life than in many other countries.[8]

The German preference for clear boundaries, the compartmentalization of space and time can be seen as further evidence of uncertainty-avoidance.

The Importance of Structure

The need for structure – in relationships, in work processes and organizations – also reflects a greater need for certainty. The concept of structure, in its widest sense, means far more to German managers than it does to their British counterparts. This was evident both from interviews and observation.

Several of the German managers interviewed spontaneously cited structure as a key to successful management. Structure was not mentioned by the British managers who all focused on personal qualities such as communicating and listening as the keys to successful management. This difference in outlook corroborates an interesting experiment conducted by Stevens, a professor at INSEAD.[9]

Stevens presented an organizational problem to separate groups of MBA students from Britain and Germany (as well as France). The problem hinged on a conflict between two department heads within a company. The students were asked to determine what was wrong and to put forward a solution. Their answers showed strikingly different patterns.

The majority of the Germans pinpointed a lack of structure as the major problem. The competence of the two conflicting department heads had never been clearly laid down. The Germans' preferred solution was the establishment of procedures. Ways to develop these included calling in a consultant, nominating a task force, or referring up to the common boss. This prompted Stevens's conclusion that the dominant underlying model of an organization for the Germans, was a 'well-oiled machine' in which management intervention is limited to exceptional cases because the rules settled everything.

The majority of British students diagnosed the case as a human-relations problem. The two department heads were poor negotiators, and their skills in this respect should.be developed by sending them on a management course, preferably together. The implicit model of an organization in the minds of the British, Stevens thought, was a 'village market' in which neither the hierarchy nor the rules, but the demands of the situation, determine what will happen.

When prompted on the subject of structure, the British managers in our study would not refer to getting the structure right in any absolute way. Rather, they would stress the need to get it right so that it exploits the strengths of the people working in it. Unlike the Germans, they did not see structure as having a 'logic of its own'. The regional director of the British construction company epitomized this view:

> One has to ensure that the structure is right for the strengths and weaknesses of the individuals within that team – so that potential is maximized. If you bring a new person in you need to mould the team round that individual to bring that person into the team.

For the British managers, then, structure was not considered something that should be respected, nor a particular constraint to change. The regional director of the British construction company again spelt this out:

> I see structure as something to use as guidance, not totally limiting what we can do. If my subordinates see an opportunity that isn't being exploited, then that's a door that ought to be kicked against. The structure is always under review – as to how we can get more out of what we've got.

For several of the middle managers observed the responsibility for reviewing and recommending structural changes was spelt out in their job descriptions:

- *Keg Plant Manager, British Brewery* 'To review regularly the organization structure and to recommend on organization changes and succession plans.'
- *Renewals Manager, British Insurance Company* 'Major structural changes in the area require the authority of the Conventional Life Manager, but the jobholder's recommendations will represent a major input to these decisions.'

One example of restructuring occurred during the observation phase. In the British brewery, the anticipated long-term absence of the production director signalled a wholesale reshuffle of responsibilities in the production department, with new lines of reporting.

Similarly, in the British insurance company, several job changes took place in the four-week interval between the interviewing and observation phases. By the observation phase, one of the middle managers had been repositioned on the organizational chart so that he was now reporting directly to the conventional life manager, though his responsibilities had not actually changed. Two of the other managers – the existing business manager and the new business manager – had swapped jobs. But this was not a straight swap: one manager had taken a team of twenty people from new business to existing business when he switched sections.

There was also evidence that the middle management structure in the British construction company was in a state of transition, with an imbalance in the number of commercial levels compared with their technical counterparts.

All three British companies, then, were more fluid in their view of structure. Changes in personnel were often used as opportunities to reshuffle the jobs and responsibilities around. There was a willingness to experiment with the structure in order to accommodate available talent and to create development opportunities.

Middle managers were allowed, indeed encouraged, to tinker with the organizational structure in order to accommodate people's abilities and experience, and overcome their shortcomings. For instance, the distribution manager in the British brewery was allowed to hive off the computing part of his job which he disliked to a colleague. The job was adapted to the person rather than vice versa. In the German companies they were far more concerned with preserving the 'integrity of the structure'.

From their career patterns too, there were signs that the German managers sought structure. We saw, in Chapter 3, that there is far greater career uncertainty in British companies. A career in Britain, like a job, is largely what one makes of it. By dint of effort, ambition, mobility, opportunism and luck, British managers believe they have some control over their careers. In Germany, career routes are more predictable:

> The highly organised career structure of German companies limits the potential for individual advancement. It is not likely that a colleague or subordinate will suddenly be whisked ahead of you or that an outsider will be brought in. This reduces the threat of competition and cultivates an attitude of cooperation based on mutual self-interest.[10]

The conformity in German career patterns can also be interpreted as a manifestation of discomfort with areas which they do not fully master. Whereas German managers base their authority on practical expertise in a given field and putative knowledge (enshrined in qualifications), British managers claim positional authority – that is, authority based merely on management status and the rather vague notions of social and leadership skills. Lane points out that the latter 'is clearly a more precarious basis for securing subordinates' compliance and hence necessitates greater efforts in building up relationships'.[11]

Thus, authority in Britain is less rooted in the concrete. Yet British managers are comfortable with this uncertainty. In Germany, managers need to be specialists. They are expected to know what their subordinates do and to provide a technical example for them – and would feel uncomfortable if they were unable to do this.

ALL INDIVIDUALS

Another of Hofstede's cultural dimensions sets individualism against collectivism. The core difference is in the relation between an individual and his or her fellow-individuals. In an individualist culture, people focus on themselves and perhaps on their close family. In a collectivist culture the individual has broader and more diffuse commitments to the community.

In Hofstede's study, three countries – USA, Australia and Britain were separated by only two percentage points, and were more individualist than the other countries. Germany's score of 67 may not seem so different from that of the British score of 89 out of 100. However, Hofstede shows that individualism is strongly correlated with national wealth as measured by GNP per capita – the poorer the country, the more collectivist the national culture.[12] If we take this into account, then Germany's score is among the lowest (that is, most collectivist) of the rich Western countries. Again, this is a difference which helps to explain some of our findings.

One theme which came through clearly from all three German case-studies was the emphasis on *Kollegialität* (team spirit among colleagues), *Zusammenarbeit* (cooperation, working as part of a team) and a *gutes Betriebsklima* (good working environment). There was a real emphasis on cooperation and team work and a preference for resolving differences of opinion through cooperation rather than confrontation.

The reference, by one German construction manager, to '*harmonische Zusammenarbeit*' (harmonious cooperation) is indicative of the importance attached to it. Such a phrase from a British manager might raise questions about the dangers of cloning, but it epitomized the German desire for integration and unity of purpose.

Another telling phrase, used by one of the German brewery managers, was '*packen wir es gemeinsam an*'. The phrase is derived from the common expression '*packen wir es an*' meaning 'let's get it together' with the word *gemeinsam* (together) reinforcing the sentiment of collectivism in the context of the company. This exhortation is often used in advertising slogans and served as something of a rallying call for Germany's post-war reconstruction. It is redolent with images of everybody rolling their sleeves up and collectively getting down to it.

These phrases were by no means isolated examples. Some of the key words used repeatedly by the German managers were '*Zusammenarbeit*' (cooperation), '*Miteinander*' (joint approach), '*gemeinsam*' (together, combined), '*Verständigung*'(agreement), '*keine Konflikte*' (no conflicts). All these terms emphasized a management approach and style which focussed on cooperation, team work, mutual support and avoidance of conflict.

Some of the following responses – to the question of what is expected of subordinates – give a flavour of the desire to promote a general atmosphere which is conducive to cooperation and mutual support:

> Loyal cooperation, based on mutual respect. (Manager in German insurance company)

> Cooperation and colleagues, that's what matters most. (Manager in German construction company)

> Working together, as a unit, only then are we good together. (Manager in German brewery)

> Conflict is avoided through understanding, argumentation and discussion. (Manager in German brewery)

The contrasting British emphasis on the individual also came through clearly in the interviews. The managers systematically took the individual as their focal point, whether responding to questions about job-satisfaction, expectations of bosses and subordinates or job priorities. Typically the British managers wanted freedom to adopt their own approach to the job; they liked work which gave them a personal sense of accomplishment; and what they wanted from their bosses was recognition of their personal contribution:

> I need to do a fulfilling job and one where I can see what part my job plays in the forward movement of the company. (Manager in British insurance company)

> The best use of my talents. I've got certain gifts, abilities and experience and I would be disappointed if I did not have the opportunity to use them. (Manager in British insurance company)

> As long as I know I have achieved what I believe is the best result, which isn't always a good result admittedly, that's what makes me motivated in my job. (Manager in British construction company)

> Job satisfaction from doing a worthwhile job within the business, that my contribution is well-recognized. The job's also got to offer some sort of career potential. (Manager in British construction company)

> My senior management's recognition that I am doing a good job. (Manager in British brewery)

I like to get the job done, and I like to be *seen* to get the job done. (Manager in British brewery)

Their responses focused heavily on the desire for self-fulfilment, the opportunity to do things their way, to influence decisions, and to acquire status.

Role in Jobs

The individualist versus collectivist outlook also manifested itself in the fact that the British managers were more likely than their German counterparts to think of themselves having a distinctive 'role', rather than an impersonal 'job'.

This role-orientation would start with the British managers dis-associating themselves from technical tasks which might somehow constrain their wide-ranging contribution. The managers interviewed consistently saw themselves as having a 'hands-off' approach and had broad definitions of their role. The British brewery's packaging manager saw his role as that of 'providing people with the means to do their job to the best of their ability'; and the brewery's distribution manager defined his as 'keeping customers satisfied and the workforce happy'.

In the British insurance company, the quality assurance manager also emphasized the distinctiveness of his special mission: 'My role is to sit on the side and do the thinking for my boss, to initiate projects and ideas, and to move the business rather than just administering it.'

Even the insurance company's technical manager viewed himself as 'a data-bank for people' – that is, someone who could direct colleagues and subordinates to people who could help them.

There was an understanding among the British managers that their role was to take 'the larger view', to act as 'coach' or 'facilitator' – but *not* to get directly involved themselves. This was emphasized by one of the British construction managers who explicitly stated that his was a 'purely management role'.

Mant is critically conscious of the British distinction between freewheeling role and specific job:

The predominance of the word 'role' and the decline of 'job' supports the idea that work is defined by the Briton in terms of relationships rather than outputs, just as education is about learning to *be* someone rather than to *do* something.[13]

Similar arguments from everyday life can be put forward regarding societal tolerance for individualism. Britons have been dubbed Europe's eccentrics.[14] Taking eccentricity as an extreme form of individualism, Britain has a long-established tolerance for eccentrics. The term is not pejorative, and in many ways, is used in a flattering way to mean unique.

For example, Britain's best-known industrialist is former ICI chairman, Sir John Harvey-Jones, well-known for his long hair and kipper ties. It is no coincidence that the British public looks upon him – rather than a Lee Iacocca or Jan Carlzon figure – as its managerial role-model. For those who consider Harvey-Jones a one-off, Richard Branson, the Chief Executive of Virgin, who wears colourful sweaters and used to hold board meetings on his houseboat, is another example.

Deviation from the norm is not so easily accepted in Germany. There is a general belief in not standing out:

Eccentricity of the mildest sort will attract open criticism. While there is an instinctive dislike of personal confrontation there is no hesitation in pointing out to someone that he or she does not meet the acceptable standards of behaviour. Policing each other's behaviour is not seen as offensive but a social duty.[15]

This anti-eccentricity is also linked to the previously mentioned need for predictability of action ('uncertainty avoidance'). In Germany there is a greater sense of right and wrong, of sticking to the rules for fear of causing confusion. There is a conviction that everyone's efficiency contributes to everyone else's.

A collectivist outlook supposes the subordination of individual interests for the common good. An example of this is in the task-orientation exhibited by the German managers observed: the necessity to get directly involved in the work, in clearing backlogs and in showing subordinates how to do things. As one of the German brewery managers put it: 'As a leading colleague, I go in and help out when there are problems.' The idea of 'doing what has to be done' was encapsulated by one of the German brewery managers: 'You also have to jump in and help those who might need it.'

Task Orientation versus Persuasion Orientation

The individualist perspective versus collectivist perspective may be one explanation of the divergent approaches to management: Germany's task-orientation versus Britain's persuasion-orientation. The overarching importance of the task means that in Germany individual personalities can largely be set aside – there is more consensus on what needs to be done, whereas in Britain getting the task done can involve accommodating personalities, understanding how to appeal to individuals and convincing coalitions.

A particularly striking manifestation of the task orientation is the German view of *Technik*. In Germany, there is far greater emphasis than in Britain, on facts, a belief that facts *are* arguments, and that *Technik* will speak for itself. In many ways, this serves as a sort of cultural umbrella which guides the actions of employees throughout the company. As Lawrence put it:

> *Technik* is also a force for integration. The German company is *Technik* in organisational form. The skilled worker, the foreman, the superintendent, the technical director are all participants in *Technik*. *Technik* is something which transcends hierarchy. It may also transcend particular functions in the company.[16]

At times, the German emphasis on getting things done, can even lead to what, in British eyes, might seem like interpersonal brusqueness – something that was especially noticeable in the directness of requests and the routine omission of an informal preamble on the phone. Directness is deemed acceptable because everyone is playing by the same rules with 'the task' serving as perpetual *force majeure*. Lane observes:

> A production-orientation is inculcated by education and training at all hierarchical levels and thus is diffused right through the enterprise. Hence it has no negative consequences for management-employee relations. On the contrary, it provides an integrating mechanism (a common language) which is so often absent in British enterprises. A strong task-orientation generates a sense of common purpose and of shared responsibility for production.[17]

German managers, then, have a positive attitude to the task. They are more likely than British managers to be driven by the simple pride in getting the job done, and the desire not to let others down. German managers, and indeed workers, tend not just to do the job but also to internalize its purpose. Sorge and Warner, in their own comparison of British and German factory organization, observed:

In West Germany, there is a comparatively greater emphasis on occupation (*Beruf*) as a foundation for the social identity of an employee, whether blue- or white-collar.[18]

The greater task-orientation of the German managers may help to explain why those we interviewed were more likely than their British counterparts to cite their work as the main source of satisfaction:

I get tremendous enjoyment out of the work. (German brewery manager)

The task is fun . . . one has fun at work. (German construction manager)

A key difference between the German and the British managers interviewed was the way the Germans associated work with fun. The key words '*Freude*' (delight, enjoyment), '*Lust*' (joy, pleasure), '*Spaß*' (fun, enjoyment), '*Fröhlich*' (joyous, cheerful) and '*gerne*' (gladly, with pleasure) were repeatedly linked with '*Arbeit*' (work) and '*Leistung*' (achievement, performance). It was evident from the interviews that the German managers enjoyed working hard, liked their jobs and saw work generally as a pleasure. As Lane explains:

A production-orientation also implies a product-orientation, that is a concern for, and pride in, a high-quality product with which the firm becomes identified. It thus evokes a deep loyalty to, and proprietory instincts about, the firm.[19]

A good *Arbeitsklima* is seen as the *result* of working well together and, as well as a *prerequisite* for it. The emphasis in Germany is on creating a climate where work rules. As one of the German construction managers proudly asserted:

We have a very productive working environment, which I have carefully built up.

The equivalent British manager is more likely to talk about having put together a very effective team – the focus is on individuals. Crudely put, in Britain, good social relations make for a climate where 'no one wants to let the side down'; in Germany, doing good work together is what fosters team spirit.

Persuasion Orientation and Individualism

The persuasion orientation of the British managers was described in Chapter 5; here we are concerned with the link between persuasion orientation and individualism. The link is best illustrated by one of the British construction managers:

> You have to be able to talk to people. We haven't got two site managers who have got the same outlook on life . . . Everybody's got to be treated differently. You have got to weigh him up, know how to treat him and get the best out of him. (All his staff were men.)

In their ready philosophizing about management many of the British managers stressed the need to find the right approach to persuade a particular individual. Some were proud of their manipulative skills, of their ability to persuade others without either resorting to coercion, consultation or even rational argument – but based instead on finding the *right approach needed to persuade that particular individual*. In order to get their way British managers need to go beyond the facts – they need to sell, to present the facts selectively and to think from the other person's point of view.

The interpersonal emphasis in British management can smack of expediency and manipulation, especially if mishandled. It can start to resemble management by formulae. This can lead to a fairly superficial interpersonal 'sensitivity' of the sort propounded in Blanchard's best-selling American book, *One Minute Manager*.[20] As one of the British insurance managers said of his boss: 'It's "Have a nice weekend" if it's Friday and "Did you have a nice weekend?" if it's Monday.' Thus, the outward valuing of the person in Anglo-Saxon organizations, can cloak an instrumental view of interpersonal relations.

More positively the attitude we have described could mean that people in Britain want to be recognized as individuals, not just for their contribution. The persuasion-orientation takes account of who they are, not merely what they can do.

SOME ARE MORE UNEQUAL THAN OTHERS

Power distance, the third of Hofstede's dimensions, indicates the degree to which different cultures accept that power in institutions and organizations is unequally distributed. High power distance, or a high tolerance for differences in power means in practice, acceptance of autocratic leaders and high levels of centralization.

Britain and Germany scored identically on this dimension in the Hofstede study, both featuring towards the lower end of the scale (35). This is interesting in view of the traditional perception of German management as more autocratic than British management.

The traditional stereotype can be partly explained by a confusion of manner and orientation. The fact that German work relations are more conservative, more bound by convention, does not automatically imply that German management is also more autocratic. Conversely, the fact that British management is informal in interpersonal style does not mean that it does not have autocratic tendencies.

Another factor which makes German management seem more autocratic than British management is that participation takes place at different levels. In Britain, participation is highly visible. It is obvious in the informal relations and out-of-work fraternization between different ranks, including managers and workers.

In Germany, participation is much more routinized or institutionalized. It is in the system of consultation and worker representation on the board (*Aufsichtsrat*) and in the stringent regulations about minimum office space and working conditions. It is also implicit in the shorter hierarchical distance between managers, in the absence of élite institutions grooming top managers – though there are numerous attempts to establish them – and in the smaller salary differentials between top and bottom; as well as the more contractual approach to work, where managers are not expected to stay late as part of their managerial penance for the sake of appearance, rather than to complete a task.

A third factor which makes German management seem more autocratic than it is, is its task-orientation. Again though, a production-orientation need not imply the surrender of a concern for human relations. It merely constitutes a different approach to motivating workers. As Lane explains:

> The production-oriented German style has an inbuilt integrating focus which provides a common basis for relationships and encourages cooperative attitudes.[21]

In other words, if everyone buys into task-orientation, then there is no need for authoritarianism to enforce it. As long as everyone's expectations are the same, then no one feels hard done by when feelings take second place to task.

CULTURAL VALUES IN MANAGEMENT THEORIES

The individualist orientation is reflected in the Anglo-American management literature on motivation, team building and leadership. For instance, in the study of human motivation, McClelland, Maslow and Herzberg[22] all focus on individual achievement. Taking Maslow's hierarchy as an example, he stresses self-actualization – realizing to the fullest possible extent the creative potential within the individual – as the pinnacle of human needs.

The literature on organizational politics also takes the individual as its point of departure. The major roots of the political perspective can be traced back to the 1950s, when writers like Dalton established the impact of politics on managerial behaviour.[23] The study of organizational politics focuses on the means by which individuals enlarge their power and influence in the organization; and the divergence between individual and corporate interests. It is particularly useful for explaining why events often occur which are clearly not in the interest of organizational profit, growth or sometimes even survival. As Hofstede observed:

> Employed persons in an individualist culture are expected to act according to their own interest, and work should be organized in such a way that this self-interest and the employer's interest coincide.[24]

So ingrained is this acceptance of politics in organizations, that several of the British managers spontaneously referred to it in interviews or during observation. For instance, the term 'hidden agenda' was a part of everyday speech; and in comparison with the German managers, the British managers were much more likely to invoke political explanations for particular courses of action; they were keener to offer the researcher insights into 'what was really going on'. For instance, one manager's non-attendance at a meeting prompted another to wonder whether this might be a ploy to expose a weak member of the team. British managers also engaged in more political speculation over the phone, and were more likely to see politics as a determinant of career paths: the archetypal comment being that 'Your face has to fit'. An awareness of politics was deemed an important skill for getting on. As one British construction manager defined it, the art of politics, 'is being able to play it without appearing to do so'.

The reduced legitimacy of political behaviour in Germany is endorsed by Bedeian who suggested that American managers differ significantly from German managers in their readiness to play politics to get ahead and to compete with peers for promotion.[25] While Bedeian's study focused on the USA rather than Britain, Hofstede's studies have established fairly tight cultural clustering between the Anglo-Saxon countries.

The political orientation of British management may be further reinforced by the absence of a strong product-orientation, and the relative disdain for industry. Mant observed:

In Britain, where the purpose of the enterprise is felt to be without legitimacy, it is no surprise that the 'career' may supplant the primacy of the work itself.[26]

Similarly, the literature on team-building makes much of the need to bring together different individuals to make up complementary teams. Belbin's work has been particularly influential in this area. Belbin identified eight types of people as useful to have in teams, from a 'shaper' to a 'plant' who provided the ideas.[27] The 'chairman' was responsible for recognizing the team's strengths and weaknesses and ensuring that the best use was made of each member's potential.

Leadership, too, has been a central preoccupation of the Anglo-American management literature, with particular emphasis on individual styles, characteristics or traits which make for effective leaders.

British management, like American management, firmly believes in leaders, and puts them in a qualitatively different category from managers. Leaders provide a focus for loyalty, they are expected to be decisive and are deemed to make a major difference. For instance, they are popularly credited with single-handedly turning around a company's fortunes.

German management plays down the impact of the leader. Indeed, the power of German corporate heads is institutionally diffused. Decisions in Germany are made by the whole management board, or *Vorstand*, not by individual managers though in some companies the chairman of the *Vorstand* has a strong influence on decisions. Gottfried Bruder of Commerzbank explained the more collegiate approach:

In Germany we are far more used to a collegiate, committee-style of decision-making. Our style is more immune to your 'star culture'. The British style, looser with much more responsibility for the top managers, lends itself to people running away with things.'[28]

This approach percolates down from the top of the company. German middle managers stressed their desire to be perceived as partners or colleagues rather than as 'bosses'. In the words of one of the German brewery managers: 'I want to be seen as a colleague, who perhaps leads, but not necessarily as the boss.'

Part IV

Lessons

9 Lessons

The lessons we can draw from our research concern the study of management work, the nature of managerial work, the distinctive characteristics of middle management work and the similarities and differences between the perception and the practice of management in the two countries.

OUR METHODOLOGY

Our approach was, as far as we know, unique in bringing systematic observational research to cross-cultural research. Previously, cross-cultural research has tended to be questionnaire-based though some studies have also used interviews. A number of those who have studied managerial behaviour have used non-participant observation as a method and have shown its value. Hence we adopted that approach to the study of cross-cultural managerial work and behaviour. We have further shown the advantages, but also the difficulties, of using a new method – that of joint observation by researchers from the two countries.

We can make some suggestions for improvement to future researchers. Where possible, it would be desirable to extend the observation and interviewing to provide a more complete picture of the manager's job and behaviour. This could be done by having two separate periods of observation, which could also give more opportunity to study the development and execution of agendas. A second interview with the manager would enable the researcher to check the intepretation of the first interview and of the observation.

There is clearly a lot more research that could be done to study the nature of agendas of middle managers and how and why these may differ. One potentially interesting aspect would be to study how the manager's agenda connects with the interests and agendas of those who are expected to implement it.

Our approach was very inductive. The paucity of reliable tools for comparing management in different countries meant that we had to develop our own. We used Stewart's model of demands, constraints and choices in a way not originally intended by the author – but the

191

framework proved sufficiently flexible to be useful for cross-cultural comparison.

Furthermore, because cross-cultural research requires macro-explanations, we had to cast our net wide, to collect information at many different levels – from the specific to the contextual, from the quantifiable to the qualitative.

RESEARCH FINDINGS

The research has contributed to our understanding of management in Britain and Germany in a number of ways: confirming and fleshing out the views and findings of other writers about British and German management; providing new explanations for established differences; and providing a number of new insights.

Differences Confirmed

The findings confirm that societal norms, to do with uncertainty avoidance, individualism, view of management and so on, affect the way that managers go about their jobs. But these cultural differences account for only some of the differences in managerial behaviour. Other contributory factors highlighted include economic circumstances of the sector or the firm, organizational structure, the type of technology, and institutional influences.

The study also confirmed the theme noted by several writers on Anglo-German comparisons, that German management is more concerned with the structure, British with the process. Again, this is partly because the concept of management as a separate activity is more developed in Britain. German and British middle managers have a different understanding of management and therefore manage in a different way.

The embeddedness of jobs in Germany was greater. The dimensions of the job were predetermined and the person was expected to meet those expectations. In Britain, there was a more developed notion of the job being 'what you make of it'. This was encouraged by the more flexible attitude to organizational structure in Britain – to accommodate talents and make up for weaknesses.

The differences in structure found in earlier studies still exist; hence the impossibility of finding matched jobs in the same functions.

Differences Modified

The findings suggest that we need to reconsider the view that:

1. *German management is autocratic:* This stems partly from the fact that it is more formal and structured. However, since all employees 'buy into' the idea that organizations should be task-oriented, there is less of a need to handle others with 'kid gloves'. Task-orientation can be seen as more than just a bias – it serves as an ideology that gives German management common purpose and direction, and provides social cement.
2. *Networking is important in management:* Networking also exists in German management but it seems to be a larger part of Anglo-American management and management literature. Networking and the constant exchange of tangential information is more necessary in the more fluid and complex organizational structures described earlier and in the shorter time that British and American managers spend in the same post. There may, too, be a greater tendency to self-promotion, which can be an aspect of networking, where position is not clearly based on qualifications.
3. *Discontinuity is the only way to bring about change:* There is an Anglo-American view that in order to turn around a situation, you need to bring in outsiders with a fresh view of what needs doing. The German example would suggest that creativity and dynamism is also possible from within, even though our study was not of the implementation of change.

Many preoccupations are shared by both British and German middle management. They each differ from top management in their respective countries, but they differ in different ways. British middle managers seem to be closer to 'scaled-down top managers' than their German counterparts.

New Insights

The findings suggest that:

1 managerial careers are markedly different in Britain and Germany. The striking difference in the amount of time that the British and German middle managers spend in the same job, the

lack of lateral mobility – both internal and across firms or sectors – is related to the perception of management and career development. In Britain, even those managers whose careers have reached a plateau, will be rotated in order to keep them stimulated/challenged.

2   what British and German managers want from their subordinates differs somewhat in the two countries. Whereas the German managers look for dependability and reliability, the British managers look for honesty. The British managers have little or no actual involvement in the work and therefore depend on their staff to be honest with them, not to 'pull the wool over their eyes' and to keep them informed when there are problems.

3   the German firms studied had greater structural stability. One explanation may be that this is a result of operating in a financial market where growth by acquisition is not the norm, so there is less need to change the structure to join new parts of the company together. Another explanation may be that greater care had been taken over the initial development of the structure, together with greater standardization of qualifications (i.e. closer match between job and incumbent) meant there was less need for change.

It is interesting how contrary the relative structural stability of the German firms studied is to the Anglo-American – and other – writings, about the need for fluid organizations. Among the possible explanations for this are that: British top managers have absorbed the advocacy of management gurus and so believe that the path to greater competitive success requires reorganization; the slimmer German organizations have less need for change.

4   the paucity of research into middle management has meant that the differences between middle and top management have, with minor exceptions, not been studied. Our research has highlighted the distinctive characteristics of middle management work and hence how it differs from the generalizations made about managerial work which have been based on studies of top managers. It is also noteworthy that, with the partial exception of the automation in the German insurance company, there were no indications in the other five companies of the role of middle management disappearing, or even being radically transformed, as is so widely proclaimed. This may partly be explained by the industries studied, but they were three different types of industries, and those who generalize about the vanishing middle manager rarely restrict their assertions to particular industries.

SOME PRACTICAL IMPLICATIONS

Effectiveness is bound by culture. Although there are similarities in the role of middle managers in the two countries ('to keep the show on the road') there are also differences in what is required and seen to be effective. For instance, the ability to be an effective networker and 'man- (and woman-) manager' is much more important in Britain, whereas the ability to provide technical assistance to subordinates is seen as much more important in Germany.

The differences between British and German managers, including the ways in which effectiveness is judged, need to be understood by all those who have to work with managers from the other country. The growth of cross-country alliances makes this understanding of increasing relevance.

More change was taking place in the British companies, this may mean that British managers and other staff find it easier to adapt to changing situations.

At least two opposing views can be taken of the differences between British and German managers. One is that each suits its particular cultural background and that they therefore have nothing to learn from each other. The other is that the differences are greater than is desirable for effective management and that therefore there are lessons to be drawn from the managers in the other country. We suggest that the second view has at least something to commend it, so we offer a few possible lessons.

One possible lesson for British managers (and for North American managers too) – apart from the often-rehearsed need to provide better vocational education – is to ask themselves whether their emphasis on managing is overdone and whether more involvement in, and knowledge of, operations would make for greater effectiveness, though this would require changes in the educational system and in approaches to managerial careers. More involvement in operations could reduce the numbers of staff that are needed – the German companies had fewer staff than their British counterparts for equivalent outputs and one explanation may be that managers do more operational work. An examination of the more simplified organizational structures in the German companies could also suggest further lessons.

A possible lesson for German managers is that in times of rapid change the organization needs more frequent adaptation. This may have two related lessons: one is that to assist adaptation managers need more job mobility, and the other, that it is possible and useful to be interested in learning from the experience of other managers and that this should be encouraged.

There are similarities in the nature of middle-management work in the two countries, which suggest that Horne and Lupton's account in 1965, quoted earlier, still applies in both Britain and Germany, even if it does have something of a British bias in ignoring the contribution a middle manager can make by being more technically expert than his or her subordinates:

> Managers talk most of the time, and mostly face to face. They seem not to be overwhelmed with paper or formal meetings. They swop information and advice and instructions, mostly through informal face-to-face contact in their own offices. Middle management does not seem, on this showing to require the exercise of remarkable powers to analyse, weigh alternatives and decide. Rather, it calls for the ability to shape and utilize the person-to-person channels of communication, to influence, to persuade, to facilitate.[1]

To that account we would add the amount of time that is spent on checking, even if the focus in the two countries is different.

AREAS WORTHY OF FURTHER INVESTIGATION

One obviously underexplored area is the shorter tenure associated with jobs in Britain – throughout the hierarchy. There are different cultural attitudes to policies of promotion and tenure and to the associated notion of management development.

Another area, on which we have only touched, is the management of change. It can be posited that the different approaches to management witnessed in the two countries have different implications for the introduction of change. The point is made by Laurent:

> When a majority of German managers perceive their organizations as a coordinated network of individuals taking rational decisions based on their professional knowledge and competence, any process of planned organizational change in Germany will have to take this into consideration. When a majority of British managers view their organization primarily as a network of interpersonal relationships between individuals who get things

done by influencing and negotiating with each other, a different approach to organizational change may be needed in England.[2]

The different approaches to management, views of structure and uncertainty, may also explain why.

ANGLO-AMERICAN BIAS

As a result of the research we have become increasingly aware of Anglo-Saxon 'managerial imperialism', particularly in writings about managerial work and behaviour. The research process is itself culture-bound as the view of management influences what questions are asked and what is observed. The mere fact that we went out in search of that thing we call 'management' has in itself an element of cultural bias. For instance, the German managers' reluctance to cooperate stemmed in part from their view of the exercise as futile, because of their specific view of management.

The cultural bias is very difficult for Anglo-American researchers, and those influenced by them, to avoid, given that nearly all our constructs and theories for understanding and categorizing management emanate from the Anglo-American countries. For instance, most management theory (on politics, motivation, leadership, even teams) has been developed in highly individualist countries. The analysis of bureaucracies by the famous German sociologist, Max Weber, is a counter-example. It is also of interest than the German 'quality of work' life programme was more voluminous than that of other countries with the government supporting projects to 'humanize' work.

Anglo-American writers on management should be aware that in generalizing about management and managerial behaviour they are doing so with a distinctive bias, so that their statements have a restricted cultural relevance. Management theories have been dominated by the individualistic bias of Anglo-Saxon management.

Appendix I
Research Instruments

Pre-interview Data from Manager

Please give us brief details about yourself and your job:

1. Age ☐
2. Official job title ☐
3. Number of <u>direct</u> subordinates ☐
4. Number of subordinates ☐
5. What kind of people work for you ☐
   (age/qualification/sex)
6. Length of time with present company ☐
7. Length of time in present job ☐
8. What were your previous jobs?

Type of job	Company	Length of time

9. Please specify any relevant qualifications and training (external/internal) you have had:

10. Could you list all the formal meetings (internal/external) you have to attend:

Type of meeting	Participants	Initiated by	Approximate Duration	Frequency

11. In terms of time, approximately how far away ☐
    is your boss's office?

12. Are your subordinates:
    In the same place ☐   Dispersed ☐

13. Do you have access to a personal secretary?
    Yes ☐   No ☐

14. Is there a variable element in your salary?
    Yes ☐   No ☐

Thank you for your cooperation

Middle Manager Questionnaire

1. What are your major responsibilities?
2. What have been the main changes that have affected your job in the last year?
3. What matters most to you in a job?
4. Do you enjoy your job?
5. What do you enjoy about it?
6. What do you dislike about it?
7. What are the problems in the job?
8. Which aspects of your job do you consider most important?
9. Do you work to targets or objectives? Does meeting them affect your rewards?
10. Do you have other personal current priorities?
11. What work must you do yourself and cannot be delegated?
12. Could somebody else in your job delegate more or less?
13. Could somebody else do your job pretty differently?
14. What would you see as the differences between what effective and less effective managers in your kind of job do?
15. Are there changes that would make it easier for you to work effectively?
16. What are the main reasons for attending meetings: those you attend called by others, and those you call?
17. Do you use *ad-hoc* meetings (two or more people)?
18. Are there formal hours of work for you, including a particular time for lunch?
19. Is there a pattern to your days? to the week? If, so what determines it?
20. What words would you use to describe what you expect of your subordinates?
21. How do you assess the effectiveness of your staff?
22. What are the main problems in supervising their work?
23. How do you want to be seen by your subordinates?
24. How does your boss assess your effectiveness?
25. Would you judge your effectiveness in the same way?
26. What do you like in a boss?
27. What do you dislike?
28 & 29. Who else do you have to deal with in the organization and for what reasons?
30. Are there conflicts in these relationships?
31. Who else do you choose to deal with in the organization?
32. Are external contacts an important aspect of your job?
33. If so, why must you see them yourself?
34. What problems do these contacts pose for you?
35. When you want to convince somebody how do you try to do so?
36. What means do you use to ease relationships?
37. Do you have to take risks in your job?
38. What do you believe in as a guide to successful management?
39. Is there anything else that is important about your job, or how you do it which we have not covered?

BOSS'S QUESTIONNAIRE

1. What are the main reasons why you must see your subordinates?

2. What are the main problems in monitoring your subordinates at work?

3. What words would you use to describe what you expect of your subordinates?

4. Do you have to make clear to your subordinates what you expect of them?

5. What are the major constraints that prevent your subordinates from meeting your expectations?

6. What would you see as the main constraints on your subordinates performing their job?

7. Could another incumbent do the job of X completely differently?

8. How do you assess the effectiveness of your subordinates?

9. What do you see as the difference between effective and less effective subordinates?

10. Do you think your subordinates assess their effectiveness in the same way?

11. What in particular are you trying to develop in subordinates?

12. When you want to get someone to cooperate with you how do you try to do so?

13. What about the willingness of your peers to cooperate?

14. What do you see as the most important determinants of cooperation?

15. How do you like to be seen by your subordinates?

16. How do you think your subordinates see you?

17. Do you have a personal guide to successful management?

18. What are the keys to getting on in the company?

OBSERVATION RECORD

Name

Position

Date

Time	Place		How Many	Method			Who (Boss/ Sub. initiated)	Comments
	Office	On Site	Tour		Talk	Write Read	VDU		

Appendix 2

Job Description of Purchasing Manager in British Construction Company

* Observe and apply Health and Safety guidelines and regulations.

* Take responsibility to apply Quality Assurance standards.

* Carry out Job Reviews for your staff, as applicable.

INDIVIDUAL
CHARACTERISTICS

The following are some of the essential skills for the job

* Resourcefulness

* Literacy and numeracy – an ability to interpret figures

* Good record-keeping skills

* Ability to work logically

* Ability to work under pressure

* A sense of fair play

* Negotiation skills

* A sense of humour

This Job Description is in no way contractual or binding. It is intended solely for use in conjunction with the Job Review Scheme, and aimed at helping reviewees to consider their jobs and make useful comments.

It is necessarily broad in content to take account of regional variations. However, it will not encompass **ALL** regional differences, and so may be subject to alteration by regional management.

Notes

Introduction

1. For a review see Colin Hales, 'What do Managers do? A Critical Review of the Evidence' in *Journal of Management Studies* (1986, vol.23, no. 1, pp. 88–115); Oswald Neuberger, *Führen und geführt werden* (Stuttgart: Enke, 1990); Frank Schirmer, 'Aktivitäten von Managern: Ein kritischer Review über 40 Jahre "Work Activitiy" – Forschung' in Wolfgang H. Staehle and Jörg Sydow (eds) *Managementforschung 1* (Berlin: de Gruyter, 1991) pp. 206–53; Frank Schirmer, *Arbeitsverhalten von Managern – Bestandsaufnahme, Kritik und Weiterentwicklung der Aktivitätsforschung* (Wiesbaden: Gabler, 1992).
2. Thomas Wagner, 'Das mittlere Management in der öffentlichen Verwaltung' in Rolf Wunderer (ed.) *Mittleres Management – leitend oder leidend?* (Zürich: Industrielle Organisation, 1990) pp. 47–59.
3. See for example James D. Thompson, *Organizations in Action* (New York: McGraw Hill, 1967).
4. Leonard Sayles, *Managerial Behavior – Administration in Complex Organizations* (New York: McGraw-Hill, 1964).

Chapter 1

1. The first major study was by Professor Sune Carlson of Sweden: Sune Carlson, *Executive Behavior: A Study of the Work-load and the Working Methods of Managing Directors* (Stockholm: Strömbergs, 1951).
2. One researcher who has explored the reasons for the behaviour of the managers she studied is Jane Hannaway: *Managers Managing: The Working of an Administrative System* (Oxford: Oxford University Press, 1989).
3. R.H. Doktor, 'Asian and American CEOs: A Comparative Study', *Organizational Dynamics* (Winter 1990, pp. 46–56).
4. W.H., 'Die tägliche Arbeitsteilung der Direktoren – Ein rationalisierungstechnisches und leistungspsychologisches Problem', *Betriebswirtschaftliche Forschung und Praxis* (1949, 1.Jg., Nr.10, S.603–14).
5. Iris Ramme, *Die Arbeit von Führungskräften – Konzepte und empirische Ergebnisse* (Bergisch Gladbach: Josef Eul Verlag 1990); Detlef Müller-Böling and Iris Ramme, *Informations- und Kommunikationstechniken für Führungskräfte – Top-Manager zwischen Technikeuphorie und Tastaturrphobie* (München, Wien: Oldenbourg, 1990); Georg

Schreyögg and Gundrun Hübl, 'Manager in Aktion: Ergebnisse einer Beobachtungsstudie in mittelständischen Unternehmen', *Zeitschrift für Führung und Organisation* (1992, 61.Jg., H.2, S.82–9).

6. Robert Dubin and S. L. Spray, 'Executive Behavior and Interaction', *Industrial Relations* (1964, vol.3, pp. 99–108); Rosemary Stewart, *Managers and their Jobs* (Basingstoke: Macmillan, 1967, 2nd edn, 1988); and Rosemary Stewart, *Contrasts in Management* (Maidenhead, Berks: McGraw-Hill (UK), 1976.)

7. Colin Hales, 'What do Managers do? A Critical Review of the Evidence', *Journal of Management Studies* (1986, vol. 23, no. 1, pp. 88–115).

8. Mark J. Martinko and William L. Gardner, 'Beyond Structured Observation: Methodological Issues and New Directions', *Academy of Management Review* (1985, vol.10, no. 4, pp. 676–95); for a review see Colin Hales, 'What do Managers do? A Critical Review of the Evidence', *Journal of Management Studies* (1986, vol. 23, no. 1, pp. 88–115); Oswald Neuberger, *Führen und geführt werden* (Stuttgart: Enke, 1990); Frank Schirmer, 'Aktivitäten von Managern: Ein kritischer Review über 40 Jahre "Work Activity" – Forschung' in Wolfgang H. Staehle and Jörg Sydow (eds) *Managementforschung 1* (Berlin: de Gruyter, 1991) pp. 206–53; Frank Schirmer, *Arbeitsverhalten von Managern – Bestandsaufnahme, Kritik und Weiterentwicklung der Aktivitätsforschung* (Wiesbaden: Gabler, 1992); S. Sharifi 'Managerial work: A diagnostic model' in Andrew M. Pettigrew (ed.) *Competitiveness and the Management Process* (Oxford: Blackwell, 1988) pp. 186–208; Richard Whitley, 'On the Nature of Managerial skills: Their Distinguishing Characteristics and Organization', in *Journal of Management Studies*, 1989, vol. 26, no. 3, pp. 209–24.

9. Rosemary Stewart, *Contrasts in Management – A Study of Different Types of Managers' Jobs: Their Demands and Choices* (Maidenhead: McGraw-Hill, 1976).

10. Rosemary Stewart, *Choices for the Manager: A Guide to Managerial Work and Behaviour* (Maidenhead: McGraw-Hill, 1982 and Englewood Cliffs: Prentice Hall, 1982).

11. Ibid, p. 2.

12. Melville Dalton, *Men Who Manage* (New York: Wiley, 1959); Leonard Sayles, *Managerial Behavior – Administration in Complex Organizations* (New York: McGraw-Hill, 1964); D. Silverman and J. Jones, *Organizational Work: The Language of Grading – The Grading of Language* (London: Macmillan, 1976).

13. Rosemary Stewart, *Managing Today and Tomorrow* (Basingstoke: Macmillan, 1991) pp. 14–18.

14. An exception to this criticism is the study of district administrators in the National Health Service which did examine many contextual aspects of the job. Rosemary Stewart, Peter Smith, Jenny Blake

and Pauline Wingate, *The District Administrator in the National Health Service* (London: King Edward's Hospital Fund for London, 1980).

15. Alfred Kieser and Herbert Kubicek, *Organisation* (3., völlig neu bearb. Aufl. (Berlin and New York: de Gruyter, 1992).

16. Oswald Neuberger, 'Führungstheorien – Rollentheorie' in Alfred Kieser, Gerhard Reber and Rolf Wunderer (eds) *Handwörterbuch der Führung* (Stuttgart: Poeschel, 1987) pp. 867–80.

17. John H. Turner, 'Role Taking: Process versus conformity', in Arnold M. Rose (ed.) *Human Behaviour and Social Processes* (London: Routledge & Kegan, 1962) pp. 20–40.

18. David Katz and Robert L. Kahn, *The Social Psychology of Organizations* (New York: John Wiley, 1966).

19. George Graen, 'Role-Making Processes within Complex Organizations' in Martin D. Dunnette (ed.) *Handbook of Industrial and Organizational Psychology* (Chicago: Rand McNally, 1976) pp. 1201–46.

20. Nanette Fondas and Rosemary Stewart, 'Enactment in Managerial Jobs: a Role Analysis', *Journal of Management Studies* (1994, vol. 31, no 1, pp. 83–104).

21. John Kotter, *The General Managers* (New York: Free Press, 1982).

22. This criticism was made by Willmott. Hugh C. Willmott, 'Images and Ideals of Managerial Work: A Critical Examination of Conceptual and Empirical Accounts', Journal of Management Studies (1984, vol. 21, no 3, pp. 348–68); Hugh C. Willmott, 'Studying Managerial Work: A Critique and Proposal', *Journal of Management Studies* (1987, vol. 24, no 3, pp. 249–70).

23. For a detailed description of the script concept see: Robert P. Abelson, 'Psychological Status of the Script Concept' in *American Psychologist* (1981, vol. 36, no. 7, pp. 715–29).

24. Europäisches Zentrum für die Förderung der Berufsbildung (ed.) *Beschreibung der Berufsbildungssysteme in den Mitgliedstaaten der Europäischen Gemeinschaft – Vergleichende Studie* (Berlin: CEDEFOP, 1981).

25. For a comparison see Nigel Nicholson and Michael A. West, *Managerial Job Change: Men and Women in Transition* (Cambridge: Cambridge University Press, 1988); Hugh Gunz, *Careers and Corporate Cultures* (Oxford: Blackwell, 1989); Regina Dröll and Dieter Dröll, *Karrieren – 10000 Lebensläufe auf dem Prüfstand – Welche Faktoren bestimmen den Berufsweg?* (Frankfurt am Main: Societäts-Verlag, 1974).

26. Uwe Laucken, *Naive Verhaltenstheorie* (Stuttgart: Klett, 1974); Hans-Dieter Dann, 'Subjektive Theorien – Irrweg oder Forschungsprogramm? Zwischenbilanz eines kognitiven Konstrukts' in Leo Montada, Kurt Reusser and Gerhard Steiner (eds) *Kognition und Handeln* (Stuttgart: Klett-Cotta, 1983) pp. 77–92.

27. Richard Whitley (ed.) *European Business Systems: Firms and Markets in their National Contexts* (London: Sage, 1992).

Chapter 2

1. Geert Hofstede, *Culture's Consequences* (Beverly Hills, California: Sage, 1980).
2. John Child and Alfred Kieser, 'Organization and Managerial Roles in British and West German Companies – An Examination of the Culture-Free Thesis', in Cornelis J. Lammers and David J. Hickson (eds) *Organizations Alike and Unlike – International and Inter-Institutional Studies in the Sociology of Organizations* (London: Routledge & Kegan Paul, 1979) pp. 251–71; John Bessant and Manfred Grunt, *Management and Manufacturing Innovation in the United Kingdom and West Germany* (Aldershot: Gower, 1985); Arndt Sorge and Malcolm Warner, *Comparative Factory Organisation* (Aldershot: Gower, 1986).
3. Joan Woodward, *Industrial Organization: Theory and Practice* (Oxford: Oxford University Press, 1965).
4. Murray Steele, 'The European Brewing Industry' in Roland Calori and Peter Lawrence, *The Business of Europe: Managing Change* (London: Sage, 1991) pp. 44–9.
5. Discussed in Chapter 1.
6. See for a review Horst Steinmann and Georg Schreyögg, *Management: Grundlagen der Unternehmensführung – Konzepte, Funktionen, Praxisfälle* (Wiesbaden: Gabler, 1990); Wolfgang H. Staehle, *Management – Eine verhaltenswissenschaftliche Perspektive* (München: Vahlen, 6. Aufl, 1991).
7. Iris Ramme, *Die Arbeit von Führungskräften – Konzepte und empirische Ergebnisse* (Bergisch Gladbach: Josef Eul Verlag, 1990); and Georg Schreyögg and Gudrun Hübl, 'Manager in Aktion: Ergebnisse einer Beobachtungsstudie in mittelständischen Unternehmen', *Zeitschrift für Führung und Organisation* (1992, 61.Jg., H.2, 82–9).
8. John Child and Ray Loveridge, *Information Technology in European Services: Towards a Microelectronic Future* (Oxford: Basil Blackwell, 1990) pp. 64–5.
9. Frank Faulbaum, Ergebnisse der Methodenstudie zur internationalen Vergleichbarkeit von Einstellungsskalen in der Allgemeinen Bevölkerungsumfrage der Sozialwissenschaft (Mannheim: ZUMA Arbeitsbericht, 1984).
10. Eugen von Keller, *Management in fremden Kulturen. Ziele, Ergebnisse und methodische Probleme der kulturvergleichenden Managementforschung* (Bern and Stuttgart: Paul Haupt, 1982).
11. Peter Lawrence, 'In Another Country' in Alan Bryman (ed.) *Doing Research in Organizations* (London: Routledge, 1988) p. 103.

12. In this respect the observation exercise itself can be seen as a microcosm of the cultural difference between British and German managers. Britons are readier to break off and philosophize, there is more interaction with the researcher, and the whole exercise is more negotiable. In Germany, it is less of a game, there is less interaction with the researcher, less scope for persuasion or insight into 'what is really going on', and less comfort with the inherent uncertainty of the observation exercise.

13. Peter Lawrence, 'In Another Country' (1988) p. 103.

Chapter 3

1. Collin Randlesome, William Brierley, Kevin Bruton, Colin Gordon and Peter King, *Business Cultures in Europe* (Oxford: Heinemann Professional Publishing, 1990) p. 42.

2. Collin Randlesome *et al.*, *Business Cultures in Europe*, p. 43.

3. Peter Lawrence, 'Management Education in West Germany' in William Byrt (ed.) *Management Education: An International Survey* (London: Routledge, 1989) p. 156.

4. Collin Randlesome *et al.*, *Business Cultures in Europe*, p. 44.

5. Charles Handy, Colin Gordon, Ian Gow and Collin Randlesome, *Making Managers* (London: Pitman, 1988) p. 143.

6. Charles Handy *et al.*, *The Making of Managers* (London: National Education and Development Office/Manpower Services Commission/ British Institute of Management, 1987).

7. John Constable and Roger McCormick, *The Making of British Managers* (Northants: British Institute of Management/Confederation of British Industry, 1987).

8. Wilhelm Eberwein and Jochen Tholen *Managermentalität – Industrielle Unternehmensleitung als Beruf und Politik* (Frankfurt am Main: Frankfurter Allgemeine Zeitung, 1990).

9. Heinz Hartmann, *Unternehmer-Ausbildung Die Rolle der deutschen Hochschulen* (München: Hanser, 1958).

10. Wolfgang Zapf, 'Die deutschen Manager – Sozialprofil und Karriereweg' in Wolfgang Zapf (ed.) *Beiträge zur Analyse der deutschen Oberschicht* (München: Piper, 1965) pp. 136–49.

11. Max Kruk, *Die großen Unternehmer – Woher sie kommen, wer sie sind, wie sie aufsteigen* (Frankfurt am Main: Societäts-Verlag, 1972).

12. Heinrich Evers, *Kriterien zur Auslese von Top-Managern in Großunternehmen – Eine empirische Untersuchung* (Frankfurt am Main: Deutsch, 1974).

13. Otto H. Poensgen, 'Der Weg in den Vorstand – Die Charakteristika der Vorstandsmitglieder der Aktiengesellschaften des Verarbeitenden Gewerbes', *Die Betriebswirtschaft* (42.Jg., Nr.1, 1982, pp. 3–25).

14. Martin Wuppermann, *Geschäftsführer in Deutschland* (Frankfurt am Main: Campus, 1989).
15. Eberwein and Tholen, *Managermentalität – Industrielle Unternehmensleitung als Beruf und Politik*, pp. 35–9.
16. George Bickerstaffe, 'Stay Put to Get Ahead', *The Times* (12 March 1992) p. 17.
17. Alistair Mant, *The Rise and Fall of the British Manager* (London: Macmillan, 1977) p. 87.
18. Sarah Strickland, 'Don't be Limited by Tunnel Vision', *The Independent* (3 December 1992) p. 18.
19. *The Independent* (3 December 1992) p. 18.
20. Collin Randlesome, 'West Germany' in Charles Handy, C. Gorden, I. Gow, Collin Randlesome (eds) *Making Managers* (London: Pitman, 1988) p. 139.
21. Lawrence, 'Management–Education in West Germany', p. 167.
22. *The Times* (12 March 1992) p. 17.
23. Zapf, 'Die deutschen Manager – Sozialprofil und Karriereweg', 1965, pp. 136–49.
24. Eberwein and Tholen, *Managermentalität – Industrielle Unternehmensleitung als Beruf und Politik*, 1990.
25. While the individual country samples are too small to test for significance, the proportional difference is intuitively convincing.
26. Malcolm Wheatley, *The Future of Middle Management* (Northants: British Institute of Management, 1992) p. 10.
27. Regina Dröll and Dieter Dröll, *Karrieren – 1000 Lebensläufe auf dem Prüfstand – Welche Faktoren bestimmen den Berufsweg?* (Frankfurt am Main: Societäts-Verlag, 1974).
28. Wolfgang Pippke and Peter Wolfmeyer, *Die berufliche Mobilität von Führungskräften in Wirtschaft und Verwaltung. Ein empirischer Vergleich ihrer Berufswerdegänge und deren Bestimmungsfaktoren* (Baden-Baden: Nomos, 1976).
29. Nigel Nicholson and Michael West, *Managerial Job Change: Men and Women in Transition* (Cambridge: Cambridge University Press, 1988) p. 49.
30. *The Times* (12 March 1992) p. 17.

Chapter 4

1. Christel Lane, *Management and Labour in Europe – The Industrial Enterprise in Germany, Britain and France* (Aldershot: Edward Elgar, 1989) p. 44.
2. Christel Lane, 'European Business Systems: Britain and Germany Compared', in Richard Whitley (ed.) *European Business Systems* (London: Sage, 1992) pp. 64–97.

3. Murray Steele, 'The European Brewing Industry' in Roland Calori and Peter Lawrence (eds) *The Business of Europe: Managing Change* (London: Sage, 1992) pp. 26–71.

4. Rosemary Stewart, *Choices for the Manager: A Guide to Managerial Work and Behaviour* (Maidenhead: McGraw-Hill, 1982) p. 2.

Chapter 5

1. Derek Torrington, Jane Weightman, Kirsty Johns, *Effective Management: People and Organisation* (London and Aldershot, Hants: IPM and Gower, 1989) p. 5

2. Jim Tomlinson, *The Unequal Struggle? British Socialism and the Capitalist Enterprise* (London: Methuen, 1982) p. 128.

3. Mason Haire, *Modern Organization Theory* (New York: John Wiley, 1959) pp. 302–3.

4. J.H. Horne and Tom Lupton, 'The Work Activities of "Middle" Managers', *Journal of Management Studies* (February 1965) pp. 14–33, p. 27.

5. Ibid, p. 32.

6. Ibid, pp. 22–3.

7. Rosemary Stewart, *Managers and their Jobs* (London: Pan, 1967).

8. Ibid, p. 39.

9. John Kotter, *The General Managers* (New York: The Free Press, 1982).

10. Robert P. Abelson, 'Psychological Status of the Script Concept', in *American Psychologist* (1981, vol. 36, no. 7, pp. 715–29) p. 715.

11. Dennis A. Gioia and Peter P. Poole, 'Scripts in Organizational Behaviour', in *Academy of Management Review* (1984, vol. 9, no. 3, pp. 449–59) p. 449.

12. John Mole, *Mind Your Manners* (London: The Industrial Society, 1990) p. 42.

13. There are echoes here of Rosabeth Moss Kanter's observation of the treatment of secretaries in a large American company in the 1970s. 'Love' was one non-material reward secretaries were supposed to appreciate . . . The idea that women wanted 'love' above all was translated into constant praise for secretaries. Women were supposed to be managed through flattery . . . flowery requests for services . . . *Men and Women in the Corporation* (New York: Basic Books, 1973 and 1993) pp. 86–7.

14. Derek Torrington and Jane Weightman, 'Middle Management Work', *Journal of General Management* (1987, vol. 13, no. 2, pp. 74–89) p. 79.

15. See also Charles Handy, 'The Quest', in Charles Handy, Colin Gordon, Ian Gow and Collin Randlesome (eds) *Making Managers* (London: Pitman, 1988); Christel Lane, *Management and Labour in*

Europe – The Industrial Enterprise in Germany, Britain and France (Aldershot: Edward Elgar, 1989).

16. Wilhelm Eberwein and Jochen Tholen, *Managermentalität – Industrielle Unternehmensleitung als Beruf und Politik* (Frankfurt am Main: Frankfurter Allgemeine Zeitung, 1990) p. 102.
17. Charles Handy, 'The Quest', 1988, p. 7.

Chapter 6

1. Max Weber, *Wirtschaft und Gesellschaft* (Tübingen: J.C.B. Mohr, 1972, 5th edn).
2. Derek S. Pugh, D.J. Hickson, C.R. Hinings, K.M. Macdonald, C. Turner and T. Lupton, 'A Conceptual Scheme for Organizational Analysis', *Administrative Science Quarterly* (1963, vol.8, pp. 289–315).
3. Henry Mintzberg, *The Structuring of Organizations: A Synthesis of Research* (Englewood Cliffs, N.J.: Prentice Hall, 1979).
4. Ralph H. Turner, 'Role-Taking Process *vs* Conformity' in Arnold M. Rose (ed.) *Human Behaviour and Social Processes* (London: Routledge & Kegan Paul, 1962) pp. 20–40.
5. Linda Smircich, 'Concepts of Culture and Organizational Analysis', *Administrative Science Quarterly* (1983, vol.28, pp. 339–58).
6. Warren H. Handel, 'Normative Expectations and the Emergence of Meaning as Solutions to Problems: Convergence of Structural and Interactionist Views', *American Journal of Sociology* (1979, vol. 84, pp. 855–81); Jerald Heiss, 'Social Roles', in Morris Rosenberg and Ralph H. Turner (eds) *Social Psychology: Sociological Perspectives* (New York: Basic Books, 1981, pp. 94–132).
7. Ralph H. Turner, 'Role-taking Process *vs* Conformity', 1962.
8. Peter Lawrence, *Managers and Management in West Germany* (London: Croom Helm, 1980) pp. 51–2; Christel Lane, *Management and Labour in Europe – The Industrial Enterprise in Germany, Britain and France* (Aldershot: Edward Elgar, 1989) p. 51.
9. Lawrence, *Managers and Management*, 1980, p. 52; Arndt Sorge and Malcolm Warner, *Comparative Factory Organisation* (Aldershot: Gower, 1986) p. 100.
10. John Child and Alfred Kieser, 'Organization and Managerial Roles in British and West German Companies – An Examination of the Culture-Free Thesis' in Cornelis J. Lammers and David J. Hickson (eds) *Organizations alike and unlike – International and Inter-Institutional Studies in the Sociology of Organizations* (London: Routledge & Kegan Paul, 1979, pp. 251–71).
11. Lane, *Management and Labour in Europe*, 1989, p. 51.
12. E.g. John Mole, *Mind Your Manners* (London: The Industrial Society, 1990).

13. Child and Kieser, 'Organisation and Managerial Roles', 1979; Andreas Budde, John Child, Arthur Francis and Alfred Kieser, 'Corporate Goals, Managerial Objectives, and Organizational Structures in British and West German Companies', *Organization Studies* (1982, vol.3, pp. 1–32).
14. Jaques H. Horovitz, *Top Management Control in Europe* (New York: St Martin's Press, 1980) p. 70.
15. Budde, Child, Francis and Kieser, 'Corporate Goals', 1982, p. 21.
16. Peter Lawrence, *Management in Action* (London: Routledge & Kegan Paul, 1984) p. 93.
17. Lane, *Management and Labour*, 1989, p. 121.
18. Horovitz, *Top Management Control*, 1980, p. 77.
19. Ibid, p. 80.
20. NEDO, *Tool Making: A Comparison of UK and West German Companies, Gauge and Tool Sector Party* (London: NEDO, 1981) p. 3.
21. Joan Woodward, *Management and Technology* (Oxford: Oxford University Press, 1958).
22. The positive correlation with formalization is counterintuitive and deserves a comment: organizations which face highly dynamic environments develop a tendency to formalize coordination processes to make them more effective, for example, more dynamic environments require a more sophisticated, that is a more formalized, planning system.
23. Michael Aiken and Jerald Hage, 'The Organic Organization and Innovation', *Sociology* (1971, vol.5, pp. 63–81); Pradip N. Khandwalla, *The Design of Organizations* (New York: Harcourt Brace Jovanovich, 1977); Alfred Kieser and Herbert Kubicek, *Organisation* (Berlin: De Gruyter, 3. Aufl, 1992).

Chapter 7

1. Charles Handy *et al.*, *The Making of Managers* (London: NEDO, 1987) p. 44.
2. Geert Hofstede, 'Cultural Constraints in Management Theories', *The Executive Academy of Management* (1993, vol.7, no. 1, pp. 81–94).
3. Sigrid Ulrich, 'All Work and No Prey? Corporate Raiders in Europe', *Director* (June 1989, pp. 98–103) p. 100.
4. Paul Marginson, Peter Armstrong, Paul Edwards and John Purcell, with Nancy Hubbard, *The Control of Industrial Relations in Large Companies: An Initial Analysis of the Second Company Level Industrial Relations Survey* (Warwick Papers in Industrial Relations, no 45, Dec. 1993).
5. Collin Randlesome *et al.*, *Business Cultures in Europe* (Oxford: Heinemann Professional Publishing, 1990) p. 159.

6. Peter Lawrence, *Managers and Management in West Germany* (London: Croom Helm, 1980) p. 169.
7. Peter Lawrence, 'Management Education in West Germany' in William Byrt (ed.) *Management Education: an International Survey* (London: Routledge, 1989) p. 159.
8. Ibid, p. 159.
9. Christel Lane, *Management and Labour in Europe: The Industrial Enterprise in Germany, Britain and France* (Aldershot: Edward Elgar, 1989) p. 247.
10. Randlesome et al., *Business Cultures in Europe*, 1990, p. 36.
11. Otto Jacobi, Berndt Keller and Walther Müller-Jentsch, 'Germany: Codetermining the Future?' in Anthony Ferner and Richard Hyman (eds) *Industrial Relations in the New Europe* (Oxford: Blackwell, 1992) p. 219.
12. Lane, *Management and Labour in Europe*, 1989, p. 247.
13. Roland Calori and Peter Lawrence, *The Business of Europe: Managing Change* (London: Sage, 1989) p. 216.
14. Hofstede 'Cultural Constraints in Management Theories', 1993, p. 83.
15. Ibid.
16. Lawrence, '*Management Education in West Germany*', 1989, p. 156.
17. Sarah Strickland, 'Don't be Limited by Tunnel Vision', *The Independent* (3 December 1992) p. 18.
18. Ibid.
19. Lane, *Management and Labour in Europe*, 1989, p. 92.
20. George Bickerstaffe, 'Stay Put to Get Ahead', *The Times* (12 March 1992) p. 17.
21. Lane, *Management and Labour in Europe*, 1989, p. 92.
22. Paul Evans, Elizabeth Lank and Alison Farquhar, 'Managing Resources in the International Firm' in Paul Evans *et al.* (eds) *Human Resource Management in International Firms* (Basingstoke: Macmillan, 1989) p. 126.
23. Alistair Mant, *The Rise and Fall of the British Manager* (Basingstoke: Macmillan, 1977) p. 54.
24. Jane Hannaway, *Managers Managing: The Workings of an Administrative System* (Oxford: Oxford University Press, 1989) p. 69.

Chapter 8

1. Bertrand Russell, *Outline of Philosophy* (New York: Norton, 1927).
2. Laurent, André, 'A Cultural View of Organizational Change' in Paul Evans *et al.* (eds) *Human Resource Management in International Firms* (Basingstoke: Macmillan, 1989) p. 91.

3. Geert Hofstede, *Culture's Consequences* (Beverly Hills, California: Sage, 1980).
4. Peter Lawrence, 'In Another Country' in Alan Bryman (ed.) *Doing Research in Organizations* (London: Routledge, 1988) p. 104.
5. John Mole, *Mind your Manners* (London: The Industrial Society, 1990) p. 44.
6. Nigel Cope, 'In Search of Euroman', *Management Today* (June 1992, pp. 50–3) p. 50.
7. Geert Hofstede, 'Motivation, Leadership, and Organization: Do American Theories Apply Abroad', *Organizational Dynamics* (Summer 1980, pp. 42–63) p. 55.
8. Mole, *Mind your Manners*, 1990, p. 43.
9. Geert Hofstede, *Cultures and Organizations* (Maidenhead: McGraw-Hill, 1991) p. 142.
10. Mole, *Mind your Manners*, 1990, p. 42.
11. Christel Lane, *Management and Labour in Europe* (Aldershot: Edward Elgar, 1989) p. 99.
12. Hofstede, *Cultures and Organizations*, 1991, p. 52.
13. Alistair Mant, *The Rise and Fall of the British Manager* (Basingstoke: Macmillan, 1977) p. 65.
14. Robert T. Moran and Michael Johnson, 'Great Britain: Europe's Eccentrics', in *Cultural Guide to Doing Business in Europe* (London: Butterworth/Heinemann, 1991) pp. 43–8.
15. Mole, *Mind Your Manners*, 1990, p. 43.
16. Peter Lawrence, *Managers and Management in West Germany* (London: Croom Helm, 1980) p. 98.
17. Lane, *Management and Labour*, 1989, p. 99.
18. Arndt Sorge and Malcolm Warner, *Comparative Factory Organisation* (Aldershot: Gower, 1986) p. 125.
19. Lane, *Management and Labour*, 1989, p. 99.
20. Kenneth Blanchard and Spencer Johnson, *The One-Minute Manager* (London: Willow Books, 1983).
21. Lane, *Management and Labour*, 1989, p. 99.
22. David McClelland, *The Achieving Society* (Princeton: Princeton University Press); Abraham Maslow, *Motivation and Personality* (New York: Harper, 1954); and Frederick Herzberg, *Work and the Nature of Man* (Cleveland: World Publishing Co., 1966).
23. Melville Dalton, *Men Who Manage* (New York: John Wiley, 1959).
24. Hofstede, *Cultures and Organizations*, 1991, p. 63.
25. Bedeian, Arthur G., 'A Comparison and Analysis of German and US Managerial Attitudes Towards the Legitimacy of Organizational Influence', *Academy of Management Journal* (1975, vol.18, no. 4, pp. 897–904) p. 902.
26. Mant, *The Rise and Fall of the British Manager*, 1977, p. 79.

27. R. Meredith Belbin, *Management Teams: Why They Succeed or Fail* (London: Heinemann, 1981).
28. Cope, 'In Search of Euroman', 1992, p. 53.

Chapter 9

1. J.H. Horne and Tom Lupton, 'The Work Activities of 'Middle' Managers', *The Journal of Management Studies,* (February 1965) pp. 14–33.
2. André Laurent, 'A Cultural View of Organizational Change', in Paul Evans, Yves Doz and André Laurent (eds), *Human Resource Management in International Firms* (Basingstoke: Macmillan, 1989) p. 91.

Author Index

Subject Index